## U.S. Fish & Wildlife Service

# Fishing and Hunting Recruitment and Retention in the U.S. from 1990 to 2005

*Addendum to the 2001 National Survey of Fishing, Hunting, and Wildlife-Associated Recreation*

Report 2001-11

I0409673

February 2007

Jerry Leonard
Division of Federal Assistance
U.S. Fish and Wildlife Service
Arlington VA


*This report is intended to complement the National and State Reports for the 2001 National Survey of Fishing, Hunting and Wildlife-Associated Recreation. The conclusions in this report are the author's and do not represent official positions of the U.S. Fish and Wildlife Service.*

*The author thanks Sylvia Cabrera, Richard Aiken, Jim Greer, Tony Fedler, Mark Duda, and various staff of the Recreational Boating and Fishing Foundation for valuable input on this report.*

# Contents

# Introduction

The *National Survey of Fishing, Hunting, and Wildlife-Associated Recreation (FHWAR)* indicates that fishing participation in the U.S. fell from 35.6 million in 1991 to 34.1 million in 2001, and hunting fell from 14.1 million to 13.0 million. The decline in overall participation is of concern to those involved with wildlife recreation, especially considering that the population of the U.S. increased about 13% over the same period[1]. While it is clear that participation declined, it is less clear whether the decline was attributable to declining recruitment of new participants, declining retention of former participants, or both. This report examines recruitment and retention using data from the 1991, 1996, 2001, and soon to be released 2006 *FHWAR*.

This report sheds light on numerous questions regarding fishing and hunting recruitment and retention. What percent of children living at home have ever been exposed to fishing? How much did this percentage change from 1990 to 2005? How much higher is the percent of boys exposed to hunting than girls? Do the hunting practices of fathers with children at home who engage in hunting differ from those with children who do not? At what age do individuals tend to stop fishing and hunting? How much lower was retention of anglers and hunters in 2005 compared to 1990? What income groups had relatively large changes in retention of anglers and hunters from 1995 to 2005?

[1] Statistical Abstract of the United States: 2004-2005, U.S. Census Bureau.

## Report Organization
This report first analyzes recruitment and then addresses retention. More specifically, the report is organized as follows.

## Recruitment
*Age of Initiation:*
The age at which initiation into fishing and hunting occurs is examined, as well as differences in age of initiation among residents of urban and rural areas.

*Trend in Recruitment:*
The trend in recruitment from 1990 to 2005 is analyzed using information on the percent of children living at home who have ever hunted or fished. Socioeconomic characteristics of recruitees are incorporated so that trends can be analyzed for different population segments.

*Participation of Children in 2005:*
This section examines the characteristics of sons and daughters residing at home who participated in fishing and hunting in 2005. Their socioeconomic characteristics are analyzed as well as the fishing and hunting activity of their parents.

*Hunting Behavior of Males with Children who Hunt:*
This section examines whether male hunters with children who hunted in 2000 differed with respect to their hunting behavior than male hunters with children who did not hunt. Whether male hunters with children who hunted pursued different species, hunted on different types of land, or resided in different areas than those with children who did not hunt are all examined.

## Retention

*Age of Dropouts:*
This section examines the age at which individuals stop hunting or fishing. Additionally, it examines how the retention rate changed from 1990 to 2005.

*Characteristics of Dropouts*
This section examines the relationship between various socioeconomic characteristics and the retention rate in fishing and hunting.

*Trend in Retention:*
The trend in retention from 1990 to 2005 is analyzed in detail. The trend analysis incorporates socioeconomic characteristics to assess trends among different population segments.

*Reasons for Quitting:*
This section examines the reasons why individuals quit participating in fishing and hunting. Socioeconomic characteristics are incorporated so that reasons for quitting can be analyzed for different population segments.

## Data and Definitions

All reported data contained herein are from the *1991, 1996, and 2001 FHWAR* surveys[2] and preliminary data from the *2006* survey. This report makes extensive use of data from the *screen phase* of the *FHWAR* surveys because these data are uniquely suited to examine recruitment and retention in detail. The *2006* survey results for participation and expenditures in *2006* will be available beginning in the spring of *2007*. However, the *screen phase* of the *2006* survey is already completed, so, with qualifications outlined below, this information can be used for the purposes of this report.

_____
[2] *FHWAR* documents are available on the U.S. Fish and Wildlife Service webpage: http://federalaid.fws.gov/surveys/surveys.html.

The *1991, 1996, 2001, and 2006 FHWAR* surveys have the same two-phase construction. The first is the *screen phase* in which the Census Bureau interviews a sample of households nationwide to locate individuals who will likely participate in hunting, fishing, or wildlife watching in the relevant survey year. The second is the *detail phase* in which those selected as likely anglers, hunters, and wildlife watchers from the *screen phase* are given detailed interviews about their recreation activities. Data collection for the *detail phase* of *2006* survey will be completed in March 2007.

*Screen* data from each *FHWAR* survey are particularly useful in analyzing recruitment. To determine individuals who are likely to participate in wildlife recreation in the survey year, respondents were asked questions about the historical recreation activities of household members. In most cases, one adult household member provided information for all household members about whether they had ever participated in wildlife-related recreation and, if so, what year was their most recent activity. Because the *screen* queries respondents about wildlife recreation activities for years prior to the *detail* survey year, one can ascertain who has ever participated in hunting or fishing, which is well suited for indicating exposure or "recruitment" into the sport.

Data from the *screen phase* are also useful in analyzing retention. For individuals who have participated in hunting or fishing at some point, there is information available to indicate the most recent year in which he or she participated. This information can be used to identify individuals who have effectively dropped out of the sport. In this report, individuals are considered active participants if they participated in the respective activity in at least one

of the three years prior to the *detail* survey years of 1991, 1996, 2001, or 2006. Alternatively, individuals are considered dropouts from fishing or hunting if they have fished or hunted at some point in their lives but did not participate in one of the three years prior to the *detail* survey years of 1991, 1996, 2001, or 2006. For example, for the *2001 FHWAR*, an individual is considered a dropout from fishing if she fished at some point in her life but did not participate in 2000, 1999, or 1998.

It should be noted that data currently available from the screen phase of the 2006 FHWAR is preliminary. It is not final and has not been certified as such by the Census Bureau, so it could change some between the time this report is published and the final data is published by the Census Bureau. That said, it is highly unlikely that the data will change enough to negate the findings in this report. When the final data is available, the Fish and Wildlife Service will publish an errata for this report if necessary.

This report was originally written without using the preliminary 2006 screen data. However, the benefit of incorporating the latest data was deemed by the author to outweigh the risk of reaching errant conclusions resulting from using it in its preliminary state. A reader unwilling to accept the use of the preliminary data should focus on the trends from 1990 to 2000. If the reader wishes to obtain the version of this report that focuses on the trends from 1990 to 2000, it is available from the author. For the most part, the conclusions reached are the same as those contained herein, but there are a few differences.

# Recruitment

## Age of Initiation

The curves in Chart 1 display the cumulative percent of first-time anglers by age in 2005. The FHWAR *screen* contains information about first-time hunting or fishing experiences for the year immediately preceding the *detail* survey year. Individuals who hunted or fished in 2005 were asked a follow-up question about whether it was their first year to participate. Using the responses to this question, one can obtain the distribution of first-time anglers or hunters by age. These distributions are displayed in Chart 1 as cumulative percentages. Displaying the distributions in this manner helps reveal what age groups are critical for exposure to hunting or fishing.

The following should help clarify the meaning of the cumulative percentage curves in Chart 1. The line for fishing indicates that in 2005 19% of all first-time anglers were under 6 years old[3], 59% were 15 or under, and 64% were 20 or under. If the distribution of first-time anglers and hunters is relatively consistent year after year, then the relationship between age and first-time anglers and hunters in 2005 would resemble the rate of exposure for all anglers and hunters. In other words, one can assert that 64% of all individuals who have ever participated in fishing were exposed to it by the time they were 20 years old.

Chart 1 reveals that individuals are typically exposed to fishing at a younger age than hunting. 47% of first-time anglers were 10 years or younger compared to 18% of first-time hunters. However, the cumulative percent of individuals hunting for the first time increases rapidly through the teenage

**Chart 1. Cumulative Percent of First-Time Hunters and Anglers, by Age: 2005**

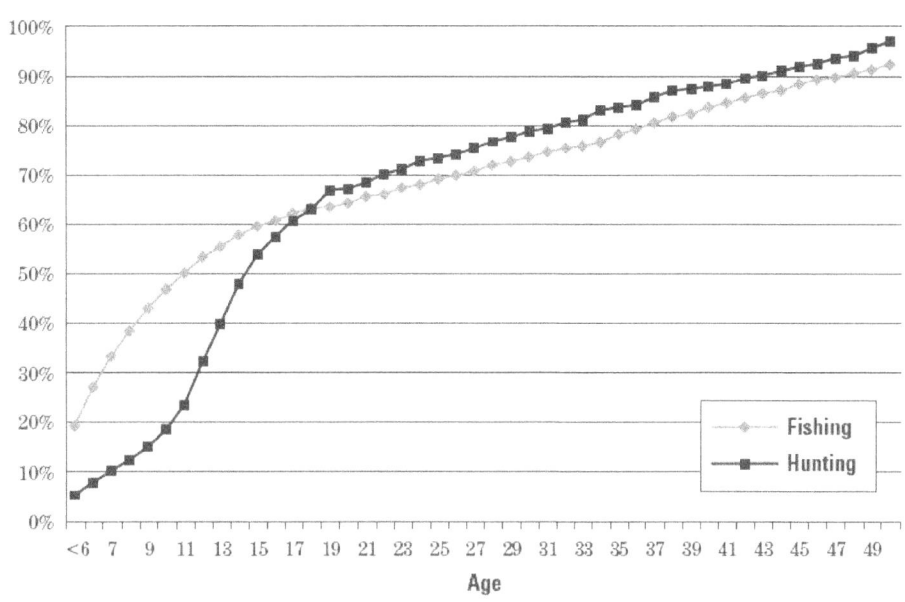

years, so roughly two thirds of both first time anglers and hunters are 20 years of age or younger.

67% of first-time hunters and 64% of first-time anglers were 20 years of age and younger. This finding underscores the importance of recruitment during the adolescent years. However, it also means that about a third of both first time anglers and first time hunters in 2005 were 21 and over[4].

It may come as a surprise to professionals involved with wildlife recreation that about a third of first time anglers and hunters were 21 and over. While adolescence is the most important time for recruitment, young adults and the middle aged also provide substantial numbers of new recruits. While this

finding may be surprising, it is also probably encouraging to many that new additions to hunting and fishing need not necessarily be adolescents.

Additional research not presented here but obtainable from the author revealed that half of the first time anglers and hunters 21 and over were 30 to 45 years old; close to a quarter of both were 21 to 29; and close to a quarter were over 45. When compared to the distribution of all anglers, those that started fishing over 20 had relatively high concentrations in urban areas, the Pacific region, and races other than Whites. They also had a greater concentration of females. The results for females indicate that they are often initiated into hunting and fishing at older ages than males.

The participation curves in Chart 1 can also be produced for individuals with different socioeconomic characteristics. Chart 2 displays the cumulative percent of first-time hunters for rural and urban residents separately. Residents

---

[3] The *screen* does not query the activities for individuals under 6. The number of individuals in 2005 who were first-time anglers before 6 was approximated by tallying the 6 year old individuals who participated in 2005 and also indicated it was not their first time.

[4] The percents of first-time hunters and anglers over 20 were very similar using data from the 2001 and 1991 surveys. Contact the author for results using the 2001 and 1991 data.

of rural areas participate for the first time at a younger age than residents of urban areas. 38% of first-time hunters living in rural areas are 12 or younger, compared to 26% of first-time hunters living in urban areas. Research suggests that those initiated into hunting at younger ages tend to have higher levels of dedication to the sport and tend to be more active hunters later in life[5]. Consequently, the finding that individuals in rural areas are more likely to participate at earlier ages than those in urban areas is not insignificant.

Chart 3 displays the cumulative percent of first-time anglers for rural and urban residents separately. Unlike hunting the age of initiation into fishing is roughly the same for urban and rural residents. Research indicates also that long term fishing involvement is associated with early initiation. If urban residents are more prone to drop out of fishing than rural residents, the results here suggest that it is not attributable to differences in age of initiation.

### Trend in Recruitment

*Overall Trend*
The trend in recruitment from 1990 to 2005 is analyzed using data available from the *screen phase* of the *FHWAR* surveys. The *screens* contain information on whether household members have ever participated in fishing and hunting. They also contain information about the relationship of each household member to the reference person. The reference person is the household member who owns, leases, or rents the residence that was selected in the sample. Thus, one can ascertain whether household members are the spouse, child, or parent of the reference person. This trend analysis focuses on children of reference

---

[5] See the following publications for more information.

Applegate, J. E. (1977) Dynamics of the New Jersey sport hunting population. *Trans. North Am. Wildl. and Nat. Resour. Conf.*, 42: 103-116.

Applegate, J. E. (1982) A change in the age structure of new hunters in New Jersey. *Journal of Wildlife Management.*, 46: 490-492.

O'Leary, J. T., J. Behrens-Tepper, F.A. McGuire and F. D. Dottavio. (1987). Age of first hunting experience: results from a nationwide recreation survey. *Leisure Sciences.*, 9: 225-233.

**Chart 2. Cumulative Percent of First-Time Hunters, by Age and Residency: 2005**

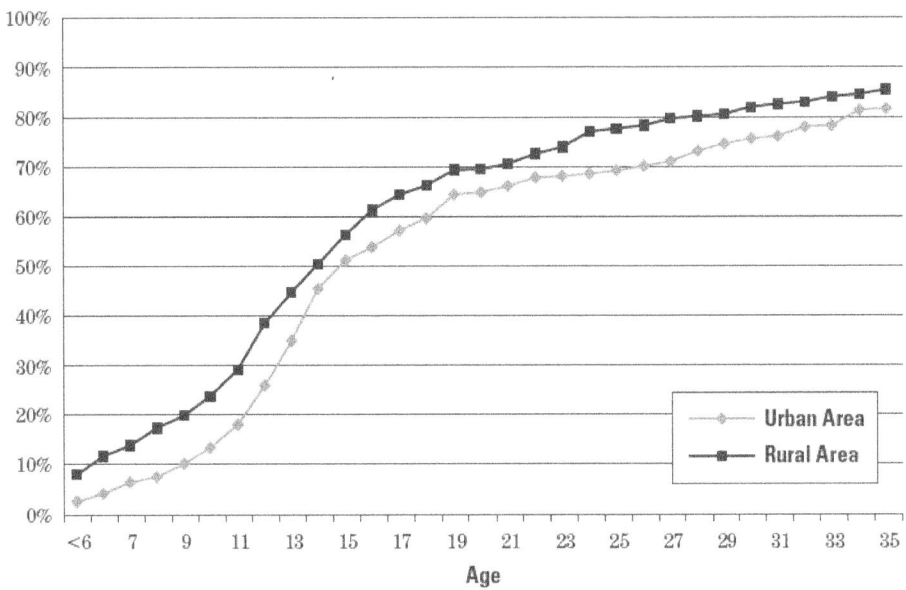

**Chart 3. Cumulative Percent of First-Time Anglers, by Age and Residency: 2005**

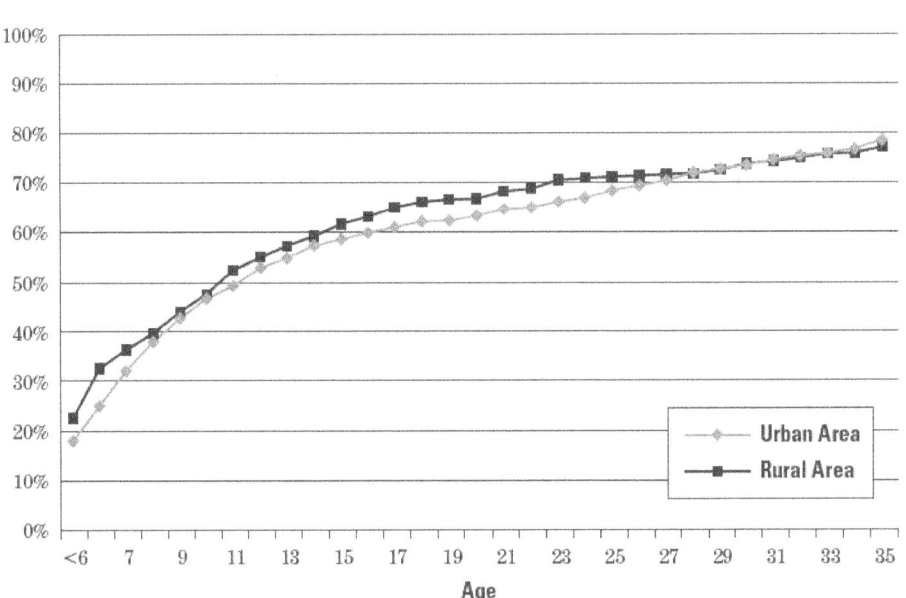

persons living at home. Given the ages of initiation shown in Chart 1, the majority of new hunters or anglers will be children living at home. Additionally, restricting the analysis to only children living at home improves the comparability of survey results over time[6].

Table 1 displays the percentages of children residing at home who had ever participated in fishing and hunting by age cohort in 1990, 1995, 2000, and 2005. These percentages represent the rates at which children were initiated into hunting and fishing, hence they are referred to as initiation rates.

The initiation rate for children of any age declined steadily for both fishing and hunting from 1990 to 2000. However, the decline in both levelled off from 2000 to 2005. The fishing initiation rate for any age children fell from 53% in 1990 to 50% in 1995 to 42% in 2000 and held steady at 42% in 2005. This pattern remained the same for the hunting rate: 12% in 1990, 10% in 1995, 8% in 2000, and 8% in 2005.

## Table 1. Initiation Rates* of Children Residing at Home by Age Cohort

|  | 2005 | 2000 | 1995 | 1990 |
|---|---|---|---|---|
| **Fishing** | | | | |
| Age | | | | |
| Any Age | 42% | 42% | 50% | 53% |
| 6-9 | 39% | 38% | 45% | 49% |
| 10-12 | 46% | 46% | 55% | 57% |
| 13-19 | 46% | 46% | 53% | 56% |
| 20+ | 36% | 34% | 45% | 48% |
| **Hunting** | | | | |
| Age | | | | |
| Any Age | 8% | 8% | 10% | 12% |
| 6-12 | 4% | 4% | 4% | 5% |
| 13-19 | 11% | 12% | 14% | 16% |
| 20+ | 11% | 13% | 16% | 20% |

*The initiation rate is the percent of children residing at home who have ever participated in hunting and fishing.

### Trend by Socioeconomic Characteristics

Tables 2-5 present the trend in the initiation rate of children living at home by numerous socioeconomic characteristics: geographic region of residence, gender, ethnicity, race, urban or rural residence, household income, and residence within metropolitan statistical areas. Incorporating these characteristics in the analysis permits a greater understanding of the population segments that experienced higher than average declines. To simplify the discussion, this section focuses on the trend for children of any age residing at home rather than the trend by age cohorts. Relevant information for trends analysis by age cohorts is in appendix tables A-1 and A-2.

For most characteristics, the trend discussion focuses on the change that occurred from 1990 to 2005. However, for metropolitan statistical area (MSA) and household income in 2005 dollars

the discussion addresses the period from 1995 to 2005. Residence within MSAs is not available in the 1991 survey, so the analysis is limited to the trend from 1995 to 2005.

MSA designation provides another way of analyzing participation by population density different than urban and rural. "The general concept of a metropolitan . . . statistical area is that of a core area containing a substantial population nucleus, together with adjacent communities having a high degree of economic and social integration with that core."

This report uses the central city designation to further refine the analysis by MSA. "The largest city in each MSA . . . is designated a central city." Other cities within MSAs may also be counted as central cities "if specified requirements are met concerning population size and commuting patterns."[7] Residents of central cities likely experience the greatest population density and are likely to experience the

most "urban" lifestyles. Hence, they also likely have the least accessibility to fishing and hunting opportunities. Those who reside in MSAs but not in a central city are more likely to reside in outlying "suburban" areas. Individuals residing outside MSAs are likely to experience the least population density and are more likely to be considered rural residents,[8] so they likely have the greatest access to fishing and hunting opportunities.

As for income, the household income categories available from the surveys match up closely when applying the level of inflation that occurs over a ten year

[8] The newest MSA standards as defined by Office of Management and Budget change the name from central cities to principal cities, but this study will stick with the central city language to be consistent.

[6] Contact the author for an explanation of why limiting the analysis to children living at home improves the comparability of survey results over time.

[7] Statistical Abstract of the United States: 2002

period[9]. The categories that are available in the different survey years do not match up well for the 15 year period of 1990 to 2005. For the period 1990 to 2000, a similar trend analysis to that presented here was completed by the author and can be obtained by request.

Before discussing which population segments have experienced faster declines, it should be pointed out that the decline in fishing and hunting recruitment exhibited in Tables 2-5 is nearly universal. Recruitment in both fishing and hunting is down for nearly every socioeconomic characteristic.

Understanding the concept of *percent change* in the initiation rate is important to appropriately compare declines across different population segments. Tables 2-5 present both the *difference* in the initiation rate and the *percent change* in the initiation rates over the periods from 1990 to 2005 or 1995 to 2005. The difference is a measure of absolute change while the *percent change* is a measure of relative change. A measure of relative change should be used to compare which segments of the population experienced the sharpest or quickest decline in participation.

An example using differences by race will illustrate the two concepts and offer a better understanding of why the use of a relative change is important. Table 4 indicates that the *difference* in the hunting initiation rate from 1990 to 2005 for Whites was –4% and for Non-Whites was –2%. The difference is derived by subtracting the initiation rate in 2005 from that in 1990, which for Whites is 10%–14%=–4% and for Non-Whites is 2%–4%=–2%. Considering this absolute decline alone, one would conclude that hunting initiation among Whites contracted faster than it did for Non-Whites. However, this ignores the fact that in 1990 the initiation rate was substantially higher among Whites: 15% versus 4%.

---

[9] Income information in 1995 was adjusted to approximate 2005 income levels. The Consumer Price Index rose 28% from 1995 to 2005. The income categories from 1995 where increased by 28%, and then were assigned to the closest 2005 income categories. 1995 income categories were assigned to the 2005 income categories in the following manner: Under $20,000$_{1995}$=Under $25,000$_{2005}$, $20,000-$29,999$_{1995}$=$25,000-$39,999$_{2005}$, $30,000-$74,999$_{1995}$=$40,000-$99,999$_{2005}$, $75,000$ or more$_{1995}$=$100,000$ or more$_{2005}$.

**Table 2. Fishing Initiation Rate for Children Residing at Home by Selected Characteristics: 1990, 1995, 2000, and 2005**

| | 2005 | 2000 | 1995 | 1990 | Difference* 1990-2005 | Percent Change 1990-2005 |
|---|---|---|---|---|---|---|
| **U.S. Total** | 42% | 42% | 50% | 53% | –11% | –20% |
| **Geographic Regions** | | | | | | |
| New England | 41% | 40% | 51% | 49% | –8% | –17% |
| Middle Atlantic | 34% | 33% | 43% | 42% | –8% | –19% |
| East North Central | 47% | 45% | 50% | 57% | –10% | –17% |
| West North Central | 61% | 60% | 65% | 70% | –10% | –14% |
| South Atlantic | 41% | 40% | 49% | 49% | –8% | –16% |
| East South Central | 51% | 48% | 50% | 57% | –6% | –10% |
| West South Central | 45% | 40% | 53% | 52% | –8% | –15% |
| Mountain | 45% | 51% | 59% | 64% | –19% | –29% |
| Pacific | 32% | 37% | 43% | 49% | –16% | –34% |
| **Gender** | | | | | | |
| Male | 49% | 50% | 59% | 62% | –13% | –21% |
| Female | 35% | 33% | 39% | 42% | –7% | –18% |
| **Ethnicity** | | | | | | |
| Non-Hispanic | 46% | 45% | 53% | 55% | –9% | –15% |
| Hispanic | 22% | 24% | 26% | 31% | –9% | –29% |
| **Race** | | | | | | |
| White | 47% | 46% | 55% | 58% | –11% | –19% |
| Black | 23% | 20% | 23% | 27% | –4% | –15% |
| Asian | 19% | 23% | 31% | 34% | –15% | –43% |
| Other | 59% | 37% | 32% | 35% | 24% | 70% |
| **Population Density** | | | | | | |
| Urban Area | 38% | 38% | 45% | 48% | –10% | –21% |
| Rural Area | 56% | 52% | 60% | 63% | –7% | –11% |

*Note: The difference is the initiation rate in 2005 minus the initiation rate in 1990, so for U.S. Total it is given by 42%–53%, which equals –11%. The percent change in the initiation rate is a measure of relative change that makes the difference a percent of the initial rate in 1990. The percent change in the U.S. Total is given by the expression ((42.1–52.5) ÷ 52.5) × 100, which equals –20%.*

## Table 3. Fishing Initiation Rate for Children Residing at Home by Selected Characteristics: 1995, 2000, and 2005

| | 2005 | 2000 | 1995 | Difference*  1995-2005 | Percent Change  1995-2005 |
|---|---|---|---|---|---|
| **U.S. Total** | 42% | 42% | 50% | –8% | –15% |
| **Annual Household Income (2005 dollars)** | | | | | |
| Under $25,000 | 31% | NA | 34% | –3% | –10% |
| $25,000-$39,999 | 36% | NA | 46% | –10% | –21% |
| $40,000-$99,999 | 51% | NA | 56% | –5% | –9% |
| $100,000 or More | 56% | NA | 59% | –3% | –6% |
| **Metropolitan Statistical Area** | | | | | |
| Inside MSA in Central City | 32% | 32% | 40% | –8% | –20% |
| Inside MSA not in Central City | 44% | 43% | 51% | –6% | –12% |
| Outside MSA | 52% | 53% | 59% | –8% | –12% |

*All differences significant at 90% level except the following: Incomes of Under $25,000 and $100,000 or more.

Note: The difference is the initiation rate in 2005 minus the initiation rate in 1995, so for U.S. Total it is given by 42%–50%, which equals –8%. The percent change in the initiation rate is a measure of relative change that makes the difference a percent of the initial rate in 1995. The percent change in the U.S. Total is given by the expression ((42.1–49.7)÷49.7)×100, which equals –15%.

To appropriately discern whether Whites or Non-Whites experienced the sharpest decline in the initiation rate, a measure of relative change is needed to account for their initial differences in 1990. This measure of relative change is contained in the *percent change* column. The *percent change* for Whites is calculated by the expression ((0.097–0.144)÷0.144)×100, which equals –33%, and for Non-Whites it is given by ((0.023–0.038)÷0.038)×100, which equals –39%. When the higher initial starting value is taken into account, hunting initiation fell relatively more among Non-Whites.

Chart 4 displays the fishing and hunting initiation rates in each of the geographic regions in 1990 and 2005. Charts 5-8 summarize some of the more informative *percent changes* in fishing and hunting initiation displayed in Tables 2-5.

## Chart 4. Fishing and Hunting Initiation Rates for Children Residing at Home by Geographic Region: 2005

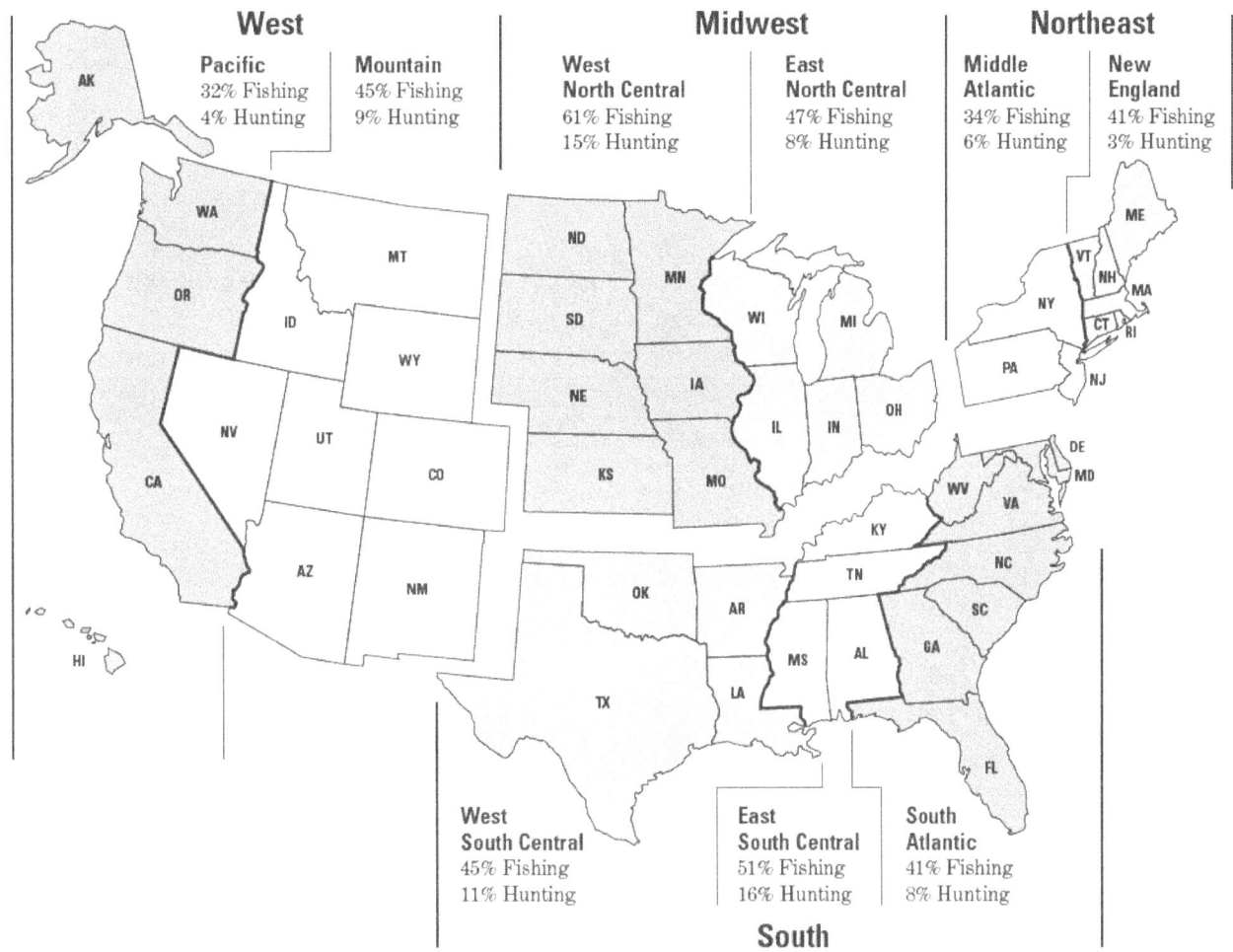

**West**

**Pacific**
32% Fishing
4% Hunting

**Mountain**
45% Fishing
9% Hunting

**Midwest**

**West North Central**
61% Fishing
15% Hunting

**East North Central**
47% Fishing
8% Hunting

**Northeast**

**Middle Atlantic**
34% Fishing
6% Hunting

**New England**
41% Fishing
3% Hunting

**West South Central**
45% Fishing
11% Hunting

**East South Central**
51% Fishing
16% Hunting

**South Atlantic**
41% Fishing
8% Hunting

**South**

The *percent changes* in the fishing initiation rate are similar among most regions, but a few regions stand out. The differences among the different regions can be seen graphically in Chart 5. The downturns in the Mountain and Pacific regions are particularly sharp. The declines of –29% and –34% are substantially higher than the U.S. total. It is also noteworthy that the Mountain and Pacific regions stand out for the decline from 2000 to 2005, as shown in Table 2. In 2000 the initiation rate in these regions were 51% and 37% respectively, and they declined to 45% and 32%. These are the only two regions in which the change from 2000 to 2005 was significant. Changing demographics and rapid urbanization, particularly in the Mountain states, are likely contributors to the change.

**Table 4. Hunting Initiation Rate of Children Residing at Home by Selected Characteristics: 1990, 1995, 2000, and 2005**

| | 2005 | 2000 | 1995 | 1990 | Difference* 1990-2005 | Percent Change 1990-2005 |
|---|---|---|---|---|---|---|
| **U.S. Total** | 8% | 8% | 10% | 12% | –4% | –35% |
| **Geographic Regions** | | | | | | |
| New England | 3% | 5% | 5% | 7% | –4% | –55% |
| Middle Atlantic | 6% | 6% | 7% | 9% | –3% | –33% |
| East North Central | 8% | 9% | 9% | 13% | –5% | –35% |
| West North Central | 15% | 15% | 18% | 18% | –3% | –19% |
| South Atlantic | 8% | 8% | 10% | 13% | –5% | –37% |
| East South Central | 16% | 16% | 16% | 20% | –4% | –21% |
| West South Central | 11% | 11% | 14% | 17% | –6% | –33% |
| Mountain | 9% | 11% | 13% | 15% | –7% | –44% |
| Pacific | 4% | 4% | 5% | 7% | –3% | –46% |
| **Gender** | | | | | | |
| Male | 13% | 14% | 17% | 20% | –8% | –38% |
| Female | 3% | 3% | 3% | 4% | (Z) | –9% |
| **Ethnicity** | | | | | | |
| Non-Hispanic | 9% | 9% | 11% | 13% | –4% | –30% |
| Hispanic | 3% | 3% | 3% | 4% | –2% | –37% |
| **Race** | | | | | | |
| White | 10% | 10% | 12% | 14% | –5% | –33% |
| Non-White | 2% | 2% | 4% | 4% | –2% | –39% |
| **Population Density** | | | | | | |
| Urban Area | 5% | 5% | 7% | 9% | –4% | –46% |
| Rural Area | 19% | 17% | 18% | 21% | –2% | –8% |

*All differences significant at 90% level except the following: Female.
(Z) = less than 0.5%, but greater than 0.
Note: The **difference** is the initiation rate in 2005 minus the initiation rate in 1990, so for U.S. Total it is given by 8% – 12%, which equals –4%. The **percent change** in the initiation rate is a measure of relative change that makes the difference a percent of the initial rate in 1990. The percent change in the U.S. Total is given by the expression $((8.1 - 12.5) \div 12.5) \times 100$, which equals –35%.

## Table 5. Hunting Initiation Rate for Children Residing at Home by Selected Characteristics: 1995, 2000, and 2005

| | 2005 | 2000 | 1995 | Difference* 1995-2005 | Percent Change 1995-2005 |
|---|---|---|---|---|---|
| **U.S. Total** | 8% | 8% | 10% | –2% | –19% |
| **Annual Household Income (2005 dollars)** | | | | | |
| Under $25,000 | 4% | NA | 7% | –3% | –42% |
| $25,000-$39,999 | 7% | NA | 11% | –4% | –36% |
| $40,000-$99,999 | 11% | NA | 11% | (Z) | –1% |
| $100,000 or More | 9% | NA | 11% | –1% | –10% |
| **Metropolitan Statistical Area** | | | | | |
| Inside MSA in Central City | 4% | 4% | 6% | –2% | –39% |
| Inside MSA not in Central City | 8% | 8% | 8% | (Z) | –2% |
| Outside MSA | 18% | 18% | 20% | –2% | –11% |

*All differences significant at 90% level except the following: Incomes of $40,000-$99,999 and $100,000 or more, Inside MSA Not in Central City, and Outside MSA.

(Z) = less than 0.5%, but greater than 0.

Note: The **difference** is the initiation rate in 2005 minus the initiation rate in 1995, so for U.S. Total it is given by 8%–10%, which equals –2%. The **percent change** in the initiation rate is a measure of relative change that makes the difference a percent of the initial rate in 1995. The percent change in the U.S. Total is given by the expression ((8.1 – 10.0) ÷ 10.0) × 100, which equals –19%.

As evidenced in Chart 5, changes in the hunting initiation rate differed more among regions than the fishing initiation rate. The decline was particularly sharp in the Pacific, Mountain, and New England Regions. Alternatively, declines in the East South Central and West North Central regions were much smaller. The National Reports of the 1991, 1996, and 2001 surveys all indicate that the West North Central region has historically had the highest percent of individuals 16 years of age or older who participate in hunting. Given that their recruitment has not declined at as great a rate as other regions, this trend will likely continue.

## Chart 5. 1990 to 2005 Percent Change in Fishing and Hunting Initiation Rate of Children Residing at Home by Geographic Regions

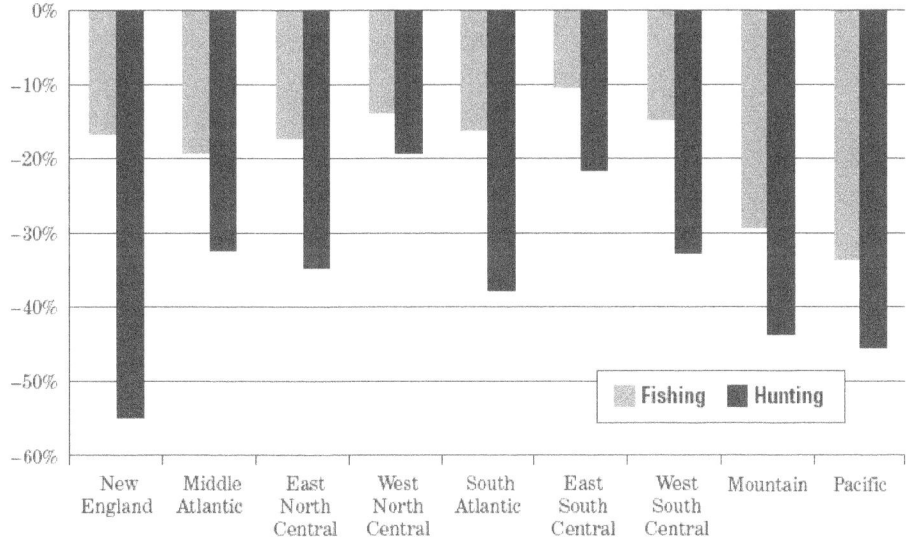

Chart 6 shows that the *percent change* in fishing initiation from 1995 to 2005 declined more among lower income groups. The initiation rate among those with incomes of $100,000 or more was down the least at –5%. The decline among those with incomes of under $25,000 was twice that at –10%, and the decline among those with income of $25,000-$39,000 was four times as large at –21%.

Chart 6 also shows a negative correlation between *percent change* in hunting initiation and income. The *percent change* in the hunting initiation rate for those children residing in households with incomes under $25,000 a year was –42%, which is more than four times the magnitude of those with incomes of $100,000 or more at –10%. The graph suggests a "threshold" of around $40,000, below which the decline in hunting was particularly sharp. This evidence certainly solicits the question of why hunting recruitment declined so sharply for those with under $40,000 of household income. Are income constraints the primary concern? Are time constraints of those in lower income households the primary concern? These questions remain for additional research.

From 1990 to 2005 the downturn in fishing and hunting initiation of children residing in urban areas was sharper than that of their rural counterparts. However, the discrepancy in initiation rates among urban versus rural residents was greater for hunting. Chart 7 indicates that the downturn in hunting initiation in urban areas was five times as much as that in rural areas, –46% versus –9%. This finding could indicate that increased urbanization in the future will have greater adverse impacts on hunting than fishing.

There is also greater discrepancy in initiation rates for hunting than fishing by MSA. Chart 8 indicates that the downturn in fishing initiation is relatively similar among those who reside inside MSAs in the central city, those who reside inside MSAs but not in the central city, and those who reside outside MSAs. However, for hunting the downturn among central city residents is far greater than those residing in other areas. Most of the decline in the initiation rate for hunting in the U.S. from 1995 to 2005 is attributable to the decline for central city residents.

**Chart 6. 1995 to 2005 Percent Change in Fishing and Hunting Initiation Rate of Children Residing at Home by Household Income: 2005 Dollars**

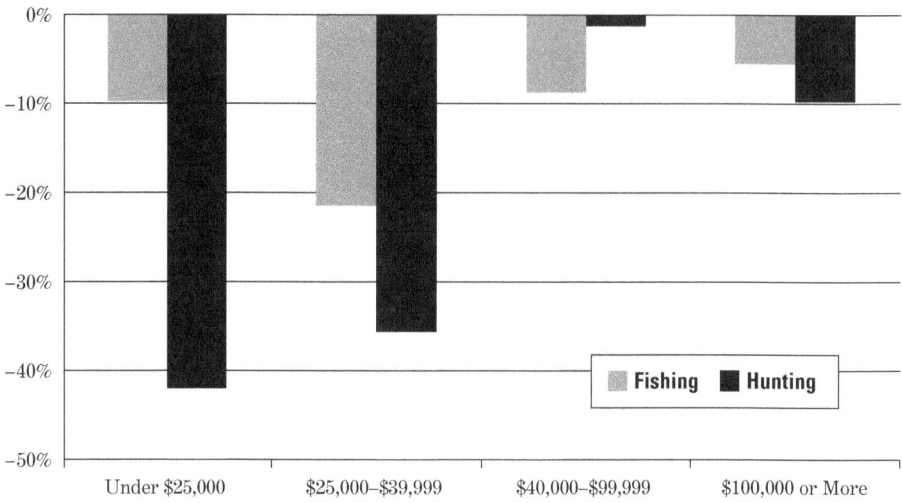

The *percent change* in both the fishing and hunting initiation rates for the remaining characteristics displayed in Tables 2-5 are roughly the same, with the following exceptions. For fishing the downturn among Hispanics and Asians was particularly sharp. For hunting the downturn among males stands out. Female initiation into hunting remained relatively constant from 1990 to 2005. In fact, the downturn for females from 1990 to 2005 is not statistically significant.[10] Why the sharp downturn for males and not females? This is a question that will remain for further research.

**Participation of Children in 2005**
This section examines the characteristics of sons and daughters residing at home who participated in fishing and hunting in 2005. The analysis only includes households that indicated the presence of sons and daughters of the reference person.[11]

Analysis of participation in 2005 provides a different perspective on recruitment

[10] Not significant at 90% confidence level.

[11] The approach of using only households that indicate the presence of children of the reference person is obviously not a perfect representation of the activities of parents and their children in the U.S. Assuredly, some households contain children that are not the son or daughter of the reference person, and they are excluded from this analysis due to the limitations inherent in the data.

than the analysis of the percent who had ever participated. The primary advantage of considering 2005 activity alone is the ability to incorporate details about the wildlife related recreational activity of parents.[12] This is accomplished by using a *FHWAR* household identification variable in conjunction with the variable that indicates the relationship of each member in the household to the person who owns, leases, or rents the residence.

Analyzing participation in only 2005 also provides additional insight into the participation of children in a single year, not whether they have participated over the course of their lives.

Table 6 shows the percent of sons and daughters living at home who fished in 2005. Daughters participated at lower rates than sons, and their participation rate falls more rapidly as age is increased. For sons aged 6 to 9, 10 to

[12] Here the term parent is used to designate reference persons and their spouses who had sons or daughters residing in their households, which will not necessarily equate to the fathers and mothers of children residing at home. There will be some adult males and females residing in households with stepchildren. In its strictest sense, parent refers to fathers and mothers. However, a broader definition of parent is one of guardian. In this sense the reference person and his/her spouse who is not necessarily the father or mother can be considered a parent.

## Chart 7. 1995 to 2005 Percent Change in Fishing and Hunting Initiation Rate of Children Residing at Home by Urban/Rural

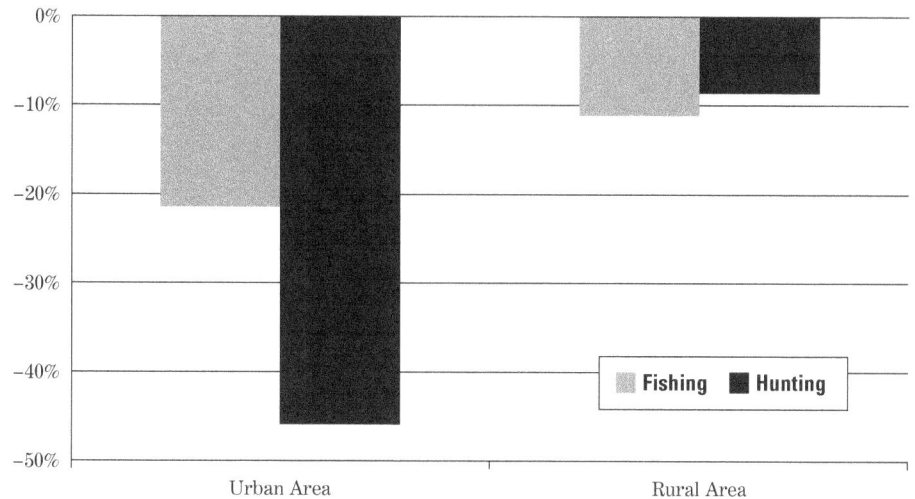

## Chart 8. 1995 to 2005 Percent Change in Fishing and Hunting Initiation Rate of Children Residing at Home by MSA

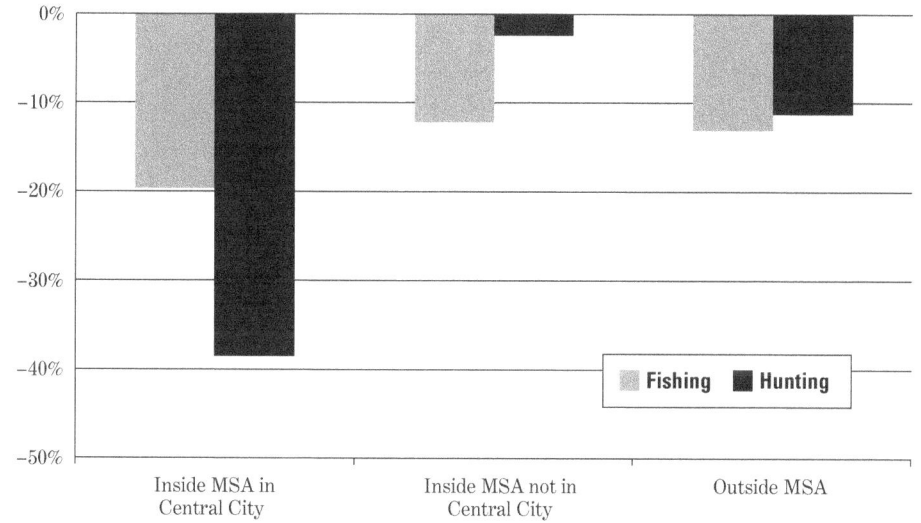

12, 13 to 19, and 20+, the percentages that participated were 37%, 38%, 34%, and 22% respectively. The comparable percentages for daughters were 25%, 26%, 19%, and 11%. The decline of daughters from 26% to 19% to 11% is sharper than the decline for sons.

Tables 6 and 7 indicate an increased probability that a given child will be either a hunter or angler if they also participated in wildlife watching. In accordance with the *FHWAR*, wildlife watching is defined as feeding, closely observing, or photographing wildlife. Table 6 indicates that 21% of sons who were not wildlife watchers participated in fishing, while 59% of those who were wildlife watchers participated. Similarly, Table 7 indicates that 16% of wildlife-watching sons hunted compared to 4.7% of those who did not[13].

Table 6 indicates that children whose parents participated in wildlife watching had a higher participation rate in fishing, where participation rate is defined as the percentage who participated. 55% of sons with male parents who wildlife watched in 2005 also fished compared to 25% of those with male parents who did not. Among daughters with male parents who wildlife watched, 37% fished compared to 13% of those whose male parents did not wildlife watch. Similarly, 51% of sons and 35% of daughters fished if their female parents wildlife watched.

---

[13] These results support a theory posited in a prior report about why individuals tend to participate in both wildlife watching and hunting or fishing. *The Relationship between Wildlife Watchers, Hunters, and Anglers* found that individuals who had recently participated in hunting or fishing had a significantly higher probability of also participating in wildlife watching than those who did not. A possible explanation that was offered was that individuals were probably exposed to both activities at a young age and continued to participate in both. The results in Tables 3 and 4 support this explanation.

## Table 6. Percent of Sons and Daughters Living at Home who Fished in 2005 by Age Cohort

| | Daughters | | | | | Sons | | | | |
|---|---|---|---|---|---|---|---|---|---|---|
| | Any Age | 6 to 9 | 10 to 12 | 13 to 19 | 20+ | Any Age | 6 to 9 | 10 to 12 | 13 to 19 | 20+ |
| **U.S. Total** | 20% | 25% | 26% | 19% | 11% | 33% | 37% | 38% | 34% | 22% |
| **Geographic Regions** | | | | | | | | | | |
| New England | 18% | 22% | 26% | 17% | 8% | 31% | 36% | 39% | 32% | 20% |
| Middle Atlantic | 18% | 25% | 24% | 16% | 11% | 27% | 29% | 41% | 26% | 17% |
| East North Central | 23% | 30% | 30% | 23% | 9% | 40% | 46% | 45% | 42% | 27% |
| West North Central | 36% | 46% | 46% | 29% | 21% | 49% | 58% | 54% | 49% | 32% |
| South Atlantic | 19% | 23% | 21% | 20% | 9% | 34% | 37% | 44% | 34% | 23% |
| East South Central | 25% | 31% | 35% | 23% | 12% | 42% | 40% | 44% | 48% | 31% |
| West South Central | 23% | 21% | 31% | 23% | 20% | 34% | 37% | 32% | 38% | 28% |
| Mountain | 20% | 22% | 31% | 19% | 6% | 30% | 31% | 38% | 29% | 20% |
| Pacific | 11% | 15% | 14% | 10% | 6% | 21% | 24% | 24% | 23% | 14% |
| **Ethnicity** | | | | | | | | | | |
| Non-Hispanic | 22% | 29% | 30% | 21% | 11% | 36% | 42% | 43% | 38% | 24% |
| Hispanic | 9% | 8% | 12% | 10% | 9% | 15% | 14% | 17% | 16% | 14% |
| **Race** | | | | | | | | | | |
| White | 23% | 28% | 29% | 22% | 12% | 37% | 41% | 43% | 39% | 25% |
| Black | 7% | 12% | 9% | 6% | 3% | 13% | 15% | 19% | 12% | 10% |
| Asian | 9% | 12% | 15% | 7% | 5% | 15% | 19% | *16% | 9% | 17% |
| Other | 35% | *42% | *33% | 35% | ** | 46% | 43% | *47% | 50% | *42% |
| **Annual Household Income (2005 dollars)** | | | | | | | | | | |
| Under $25,000 | 13% | 14% | 15% | 14% | 7% | 22% | 21% | 23% | 25% | 16% |
| $25-$49,999 | 20% | 25% | 27% | 17% | 11% | 33% | 34% | 37% | 33% | 26% |
| $50-$74,999 | 24% | 33% | 33% | 21% | 9% | 39% | 44% | 42% | 41% | 26% |
| $75,000-$99,999 | 28% | 35% | 35% | 23% | 18% | 43% | 49% | 48% | 43% | 31% |
| $100,000 or More | 29% | 35% | 35% | 27% | 22% | 43% | 51% | 53% | 40% | 29% |
| **Metropolitan Statistical Area** | | | | | | | | | | |
| Inside MSA in Central City | 14% | 20% | 17% | 12% | 9% | 21% | 23% | 30% | 22% | 12% |
| Inside MSA not in Central City | 22% | 27% | 28% | 21% | 11% | 34% | 40% | 40% | 35% | 23% |
| Outside MSA | 25% | 26% | 34% | 24% | 13% | 47% | 51% | 49% | 48% | 38% |
| **Population Density** | | | | | | | | | | |
| Urban Area | 17% | 22% | 23% | 16% | 10% | 28% | 31% | 35% | 28% | 18% |
| Rural Area | 30% | 33% | 37% | 31% | 15% | 49% | 54% | 50% | 52% | 37% |
| **Wildlife Watching Activities** | | | | | | | | | | |
| Not Watcher | 12% | 14% | 14% | 12% | 7% | 21% | 21% | 23% | 23% | 17% |
| Wildlife Watcher | 40% | 46% | 48% | 38% | 23% | 59% | 61% | 65% | 60% | 45% |

*Estimate based on small sample size.
**Sample Size too small to report data reliably.

## Table 6. Percent of Sons and Daughters Living at Home who Fished in 2005 by Age Cohort (continued)

| | Daughters | | | | | Sons | | | | |
|---|---|---|---|---|---|---|---|---|---|---|
| | Any Age | 6 to 9 | 10 to 12 | 13 to 19 | 20+ | Any Age | 6 to 9 | 10 to 12 | 13 to 19 | 20+ |
| **Male Parent's Wildlife Watching** | | | | | | | | | | |
| Not Watcher | 13% | 16% | 17% | 12% | 8% | 25% | 26% | 30% | 25% | 18% |
| Wildlife Watcher | 37% | 45% | 43% | 35% | 22% | 55% | 58% | 62% | 55% | 41% |
| **Female Parent's Wildlife Watching** | | | | | | | | | | |
| Not Watcher | 15% | 18% | 18% | 14% | 9% | 27% | 29% | 33% | 27% | 20% |
| Wildlife Watcher | 35% | 42% | 43% | 32% | 20% | 51% | 56% | 60% | 51% | 38% |
| **Male Parent's Fishing, days** | | | | | | | | | | |
| None | 5% | 7% | 6% | 4% | 2% | 11% | 11% | 13% | 12% | 9% |
| 1 to 3 | 49% | 61% | 50% | 47% | 29% | 67% | 69% | 74% | 66% | 51% |
| 4 to 9 | 53% | 56% | 64% | 50% | 40% | 77% | 78% | 85% | 77% | 65% |
| 10 to 19 | 54% | 66% | 62% | 50% | 39% | 77% | 78% | 79% | 74% | 76% |
| 20 to 29 | 65% | 63% | 77% | 61% | *57% | 86% | 89% | 92% | 83% | 82% |
| 30 or more | 62% | 72% | 74% | 56% | 46% | 81% | 85% | 82% | 84% | 70% |
| **Female Parent's Fishing, days** | | | | | | | | | | |
| None | 9% | 11% | 13% | 9% | 4% | 22% | 24% | 26% | 23% | 16% |
| 1 to 3 | 71% | 79% | 74% | 67% | 51% | 75% | 69% | 85% | 75% | 67% |
| 4 to 9 | 75% | 80% | 84% | 75% | 55% | 88% | 88% | 95% | 88% | 80% |
| 10 to 19 | 77% | 80% | 81% | 77% | 63% | 86% | 88% | 78% | 90% | 82% |
| 20 to 29 | 74% | 68% | 84% | 77% | *67% | 93% | 93% | 96% | 92% | *92% |
| 30 or more | 76% | 88% | 85% | 68% | *57% | 85% | 88% | 76% | 90% | 82% |
| **Marital Status of Parents in Household** | | | | | | | | | | |
| Married | 22% | 26% | 26% | 21% | 12% | 35% | 38% | 41% | 36% | 25% |
| Divorced | 19% | 22% | 31% | 18% | 11% | 33% | 41% | 36% | 34% | 21% |
| Never married | 11% | *15% | *16% | *10% | ** | 16% | 21% | 18% | 16% | *10% |

*Estimate based on small sample size.
**Sample Size too small to report data reliably.

Table 7 indicates that children of wildlife-watching parents also had a higher participation rate in hunting. 16.4% of sons and 5% of daughters with male wildlife-watching parents also participated in hunting. These percentages compare to 5.3% and 0.8% of those with male parents who did not wildlife watch. Similarly, 13.6% of sons and 4.2% daughters hunted if their female parents wildlife watched.

Perhaps the most interesting information in Tables 6 and 7 concern the fishing and hunting activity of parents with children who participated. If a male parent did not participate in any fishing in 2005,

the percentage of sons who participated was one third the U.S. total for any age son, which serves as an average. The percentage of sons who participated with male parents who did not participate at least one day was 11%, compared to the U.S. percentage of 33%. This indicates that if a boy's male parent did not fish at all, he was three times less likely to fish than the U.S. average. For daughters the discrepancy is even greater. Only five percent of daughters of any age participated in fishing when their male parents did not. This compares to a national average that is four times greater at 20%.

## Table 7. Percent of Sons and Daughters Living at Home who Hunted in 2005 by Age Cohort

| | Daughters | Sons | | | |
|---|---|---|---|---|---|
| | Any Age | Any Age | 6 to 12 | 13 to 19 | 20+ |
| **U.S. Total** | 2.0% | 8.2% | 4.9% | 12.0% | 8.0% |
| **Geographic Regions** | | | | | |
| New England | 0.4% | 2.6% | ** | 4.4% | *2.8% |
| Middle Atlantic | 1.7% | 5.3% | ** | 8.6% | *7.2% |
| East North Central | 2.8% | 8.1% | *3.2% | 12.5% | 9.9% |
| West North Central | 4.6% | 16.6% | 6.6% | 26.9% | 14.8% |
| South Atlantic | 1.3% | 7.3% | 5.8% | 8.5% | 7.9% |
| East South Central | 3.5% | 18.3% | 13.6% | 23.0% | 18.0% |
| West South Central | 3.1% | 13.4% | 11.3% | 19.4% | *7.8% |
| Mountain | 1.8% | 7.3% | 4.4% | 9.6% | 10.0% |
| Pacific | *0.5% | 3.6% | *1.6% | 6.1% | *2.9% |
| **Ethnicity** | | | | | |
| Non-Hispanic | 2.4% | 9.3% | 5.8% | 13.8% | 8.6% |
| Hispanic | ** | 2.6% | *1.0% | *3.8% | *4.1% |
| **Race** | | | | | |
| White | 2.4% | 9.9% | 6.0% | 14.3% | 9.7% |
| Non-White | *0.5% | 1.8% | *0.4% | 3.0% | *2.4% |
| **Annual Household Income (2005 dollars)** | | | | | |
| Under $25,000 | *0.8% | 3.1% | *1.9% | 4.9% | *2.6% |
| $25-$49,999 | 1.8% | 7.8% | 4.2% | 12.0% | 8.6% |
| $50-$74,999 | 3.0% | 12.4% | 7.7% | 18.9% | 10.3% |
| $75,000-$99,999 | 2.6% | 11.1% | 6.6% | 15.5% | 13.1% |
| $100,000 or More | 2.7% | 9.3% | 6.3% | 11.5% | 11.4% |
| **Metropolitan Statistical Area** | | | | | |
| Inside MSA in Central City | 0.9% | 3.4% | 2.3% | 5.0% | 3.1% |
| Inside MSA not in Central City | 1.8% | 7.2% | 4.1% | 10.5% | 7.7% |
| Outside MSA | 4.7% | 19.5% | 12.2% | 27.9% | 18.2% |
| **Population Density** | | | | | |
| Urban Area | 0.9% | 4.4% | 2.4% | 6.8% | 4.2% |
| Rural Area | 5.7% | 20.3% | 13.1% | 27.4% | 20.8% |
| **Wildlife Watching Activities** | | | | | |
| Not Watcher | 0.8% | 4.7% | 1.9% | 7.2% | 5.3% |
| Wildlife Watcher | 4.8% | 16.0% | 9.8% | 23.8% | 19.8% |

*Estimate based on small sample size.
**Sample size too small to report data reliably.

| | Daughters | Sons | | | |
|---|---|---|---|---|---|
| | Any Age | Any Age | 6 to 12 | 13 to 19 | 20+ |
| **Male Parent's Wildlife Watching** | | | | | |
| Not Watcher | 0.8% | 5.3% | 2.6% | 7.9% | 5.9% |
| Wildlife Watcher | 5.0% | 16.4% | 9.9% | 23.4% | 17.6% |
| **Female Parent's Wildlife Watching** | | | | | |
| Not Watcher | 1.3% | 7.0% | 4.0% | 10.8% | 6.6% |
| Wildlife Watcher | 4.2% | 13.6% | 7.9% | 18.8% | 16.3% |
| **Male Parent's Hunting, days** | | | | | |
| None | 0.3% | 2.9% | 1.0% | 4.6% | 4.2% |
| 1 to 3 | *8.7% | 27.1% | *17.4% | 38.4% | 32.3% |
| 4 to 9 | 7.8% | 33.6% | 14.5% | 45.8% | 57.4% |
| 10 to 19 | 13.4% | 46.1% | 22.5% | 65.9% | 40.9% |
| 20 to 29 | 19.0% | 57.0% | 40.7% | 75.3% | 63.6% |
| 30 or more | 26.0% | 61.2% | 49.8% | 73.3% | *66.7% |
| **Female Parent's Hunting, days** | | | | | |
| None | 1.3% | 6.8% | 3.5% | 10.3% | 7.2% |
| 1 to 9 | 34.6% | 63.3% | *54.9% | 69.4% | *74.2% |
| 10 to 19 | *50.0% | 63.8% | *52.5% | *81.5% | ** |
| 20 or more | *37.5% | 60.2% | ** | 82.1% | ** |
| **Marital Status of Parents in Household** | | | | | |
| Married | 2.2% | 9.1% | 5.1% | 13.3% | 9.7% |
| Divorced | 1.9% | 7.6% | 6.3% | 10.7% | 4.8% |
| Never married | *0.7% | *1.4% | ** | ** | ** |

*Estimate based on small sample size.
**Sample size too small to report data reliably.

Table 7 indicates that activity on the part of the male parent likely has an even greater impact on the participation of children in hunting than fishing. Less than one half of one percent of daughters hunted if a male parent in the household did not. For sons, only 2.9% hunted if their male parents did not. The participation rate for sons whose male parents hunted 1-3 days is eight times the rate of those whose male parents did not. These results underscore the importance of the parental involvement in the initiation of children into hunting.

For most parental frequency levels, participation on the part of the female parents resulted in higher participation rates of both sons and daughters than the same level of activity on the part of the male parents. If a female parent fished 1 to 3 days 71% of daughters and 75% of sons participated. If a female parent fished more than 30 days 76% of daughters and 85% of sons participated. Similarly, if a female parent hunted 1-9 days, 34.6% of daughters and 63.3% of sons participated. These results indicate that if a female parent participated in fishing or hunting then the children were even more likely to participate than if male parents participated[14]. This implies that male parents are more likely to engage in fishing and hunting without their children. When female parents go, they are more likely to go with their children.

Table 8 reveals more information about the roles that female and male parents play in the introduction of children to fishing and hunting. It shows the percent of children who participated in fishing and hunting by parental participation. 8% of daughters living at home who fished in 2005 were from households without parental participation. 15% of sons who fished did not have parents who participated. Similarly, for hunting 8% of daughters and 22% of sons were from households without parental participation. Closer inspection of the data reveals that those children who participated that did not have parents in the household who also participated were older children in their teens and early twenties. Some also likely had parents or other relatives who did not reside in the household who did participate.

Table 8 also indicates that few child participants were from households where a female parent fished or hunted when a male parent did not. 14% of daughters and 10% of sons who fished were from households in which only a female parent participated. This compares to only 4% daughters and sons who participated in hunting. Conversely, 33% of daughters and 42% of sons who fished were from households in which only the male parent participated. This compares to 65% of daughters and sons who hunted.

Also interesting is that the majority of daughters who fished included a female parent who participated. 45% were from households where both parents fished

and 14% were from households where only the female parent participated. Taken together this indicates that 59% of all daughters who fished were from households with a female parent who fished. 43% of sons were from households in which a female parent participated. This likely indicates that activity of the female parent is more critical to the participation of daughters in fishing than sons.

Closer inspection of the data in Tables 6 and 7 reveals that increased avidity on the part of the male parent had a different impact on the percent of children who participated in fishing than it had on hunting. Chart 9 reveals that even if the male parent only fished a few days, the participation rates of children increased dramatically. When a male parent in the household fished 1-3 days the participation rate of sons increased from 11% to 67% and the rate for daughters from 5% to 49%.

Although participation rates continue to climb as the male parent's fishing days increase, the changes between each frequency stage are slight in comparison to the dramatic change that occurs between no participation and 1-3 days of participation. Some activity on the part of the male parent, even if slight, appears important to the participation of children.

Chart 10 reveals that the participation rates of children in hunting are highly responsive to the participation frequency of male parents. Increased frequency of participation of the male parent was associated with steady and sizeable gains in the participation rates of children. When male parents participated 1-3 days, 10-19 days, and 30 or more days, the participation rate of sons climbed from 27% to 46% to 61%, and the participation rate for daughters climbed from 9% to 13% to 26%.

A lingering question related to hunting and fishing among children is whether their parents' marital status affects participation. This issue can be analyzed using FHWAR data with some definitional limitations. In the context of the survey and this analysis, children are considered to be from divorced households if the parent with whom they live was divorced at the time of the survey. Those children from households with parents who were divorced prior to the survey but at the time of the survey lived with a parent who remarried are considered to be from married households. Additionally, children from divorced households are considered from single parent households at the time of the survey provided no other non-marital cohabitant is considered a parent. The survey did not determine if other unmarried cohabitants were present in the household.

Considering the definitional limitations described above, Tables 6 and 7 reveal that there are slight differences in participation rates of sons and daughters from married households and divorced households. However, none of these differences are statistically significant.[15] Lack of a statistical significance means that there is greater than 10% chance that the differences shown could have occurred by chance. This analysis was also done using data from the 2001 survey. In all but one case the differences were not statistically significant there either. The only difference in the participation rate between any age children from married versus divorced households was for daughters fishing.

---

[15] At 90% confidence level.

---

[14] For several categories of parental frequency, activity on the part of the female parent does not result in significantly higher participation rate of children than the same frequency on the part of the male parent. There is no significant difference in hunting participation rate of sons and daughters whose female parents hunted 20 to 29 days than those whose male parents hunted 20 to 29 days. There is no significant difference among sons whose male versus female parents hunted 30 days or more. Sons whose female parent fished 10 to 19 days were not significantly more likely to participate in fishing than those with fathers who fished 10 to 19 days.

**Table 8. Distribution of Sons and Daughters Living at Home Who Fished and Hunted in 2005 by Parents' Activity**

| | Fishing | | Hunting | |
| --- | --- | --- | --- | --- |
| | *Daughters* | *Sons* | *Daughters* | *Sons* |
| Without parents who go | 8% | 15% | 8% | 22% |
| Male and female parents both go | 45% | 33% | 23% | 10% |
| Male parent goes; female parent doesn't | 33% | 42% | 65% | 65% |
| Female parent goes; male parent doesn't | 14% | 10% | 4% | 4% |
| Total | 100% | 100% | 100% | 100% |

**Chart 9. Percent of Sons and Daughters Residing at Home who Participated in Fishing by Male Parents' Days of Fishing: 2005**

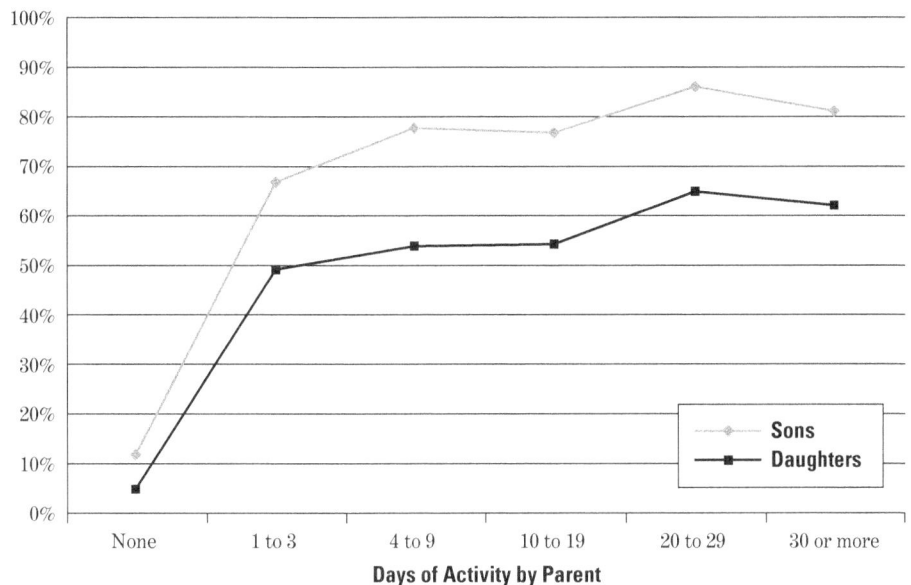

**Days of Activity by Parent**

**Chart 10. Percent of Sons and Daughters Residing at Home who Participated in Hunting by Male Parents' Days of Hunting: 2005**

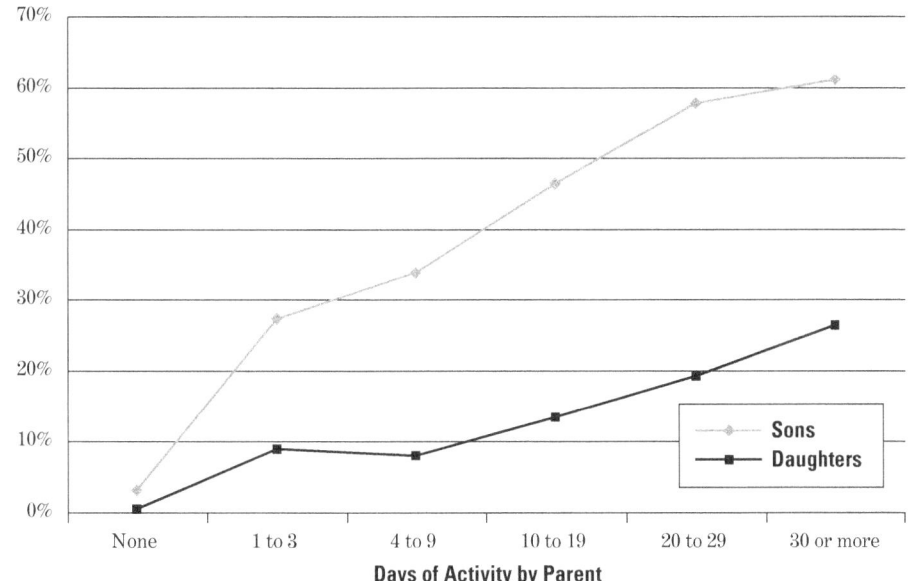

**Days of Activity by Parent**

## Hunting Behavior of Males with Children who Hunt

Data from the *detail phase* and *screen phase* of the 2001 *FHWAR* were merged to analyze how the hunting practices of men with children in the same household who hunted differed from those practices of men whose children in the household did not hunt. This analysis cannot be performed yet with data from the 2006 survey, because the detail phase has not been completed. The *screen* data contains information about households with children and whether those children hunted or fished in 2000. The *detail* data contains information about the fishing and hunting activities of individuals identified as likely hunters and anglers in the *screen phase*. Among other things, the *detail* data contain information about the species of game and fish pursued, type of land used for fishing and hunting (i.e., public, private, leased), and expenditures made on fishing and hunting trips and equipment[16].

By merging the *detail* and *screen* data together, one can answer several questions of interest about whether the hunting activities of males with children who hunted differ from those of males with children who did not hunt. For example, we can examine whether male hunters with children who hunted pursued different species than those with children who did not hunt. The answer should provide some insight into species pursued when introducing a child to hunting. These species are referred to as "introductory species." Additionally, one can examine whether male hunters with children who hunted were more prone to hunt on private land or public land, whether they were more prone to live in rural areas or large metropolitan areas, and whether they were more prone to have higher incomes.

For the purposes of this section, the qualifying language "in the household" has been removed for simplicity. Thus, "men without children" refers to "men without children in the household."

[16] It is important to note that activities of the children are for year 2000 only, and the activities of those males with children residing at home are for 2001. Consequently, there is not perfect comparability between the children and parent data. It would be preferable to have data for the parents and children correspond to the same year of activity.

## Species Pursued by Male Hunters with Children

Table 9 presents male hunters by species pursued and whether they had children who hunted. Beside each column of the number of hunters is a percent column that indicates the percent of those hunters who pursued the species named by the row. Thus, the second row and second column indicates that 84% of all male hunters pursued big game. The second row and last column indicates that 88% of male hunters pursued big game if they had children who hunted. The percent columns permit one to ascertain if males with children who hunted pursued a particular species more than males with children who did not hunt or those without children.

Comparing the percentages reveals that men with children who hunted had relativity high concentrations in species in which small caliber rifles or shotguns are used. 27% of men with children who hunted pursued turkey, compared to 14% of those with children who did not hunt and 20% of those without children. 51% of men with children who hunted pursued small game, compared to 38% of those with children who did not hunt and 43% of those without children. Rabbit and squirrel are small game species where the difference between the percent of men with children who hunted and those who did not hunt are particularly high. For squirrel, the percentage of hunters with children who hunted is more than double that of those with children who did

not hunt. Men with children who hunted are also more prone to participate in migratory bird hunting.

It is perhaps not surprising to find evidence suggesting that small game and migratory birds serve important roles as introductory species to initiate children into hunting. The weapons used for these species are probably a contributing factor. Small caliber rifles and shotguns are typical firearms of choice for hunting these species. They produce recoil levels that children can more easily accommodate than those produced by high powered rifles used in big game hunting. Additionally, these firearms have relatively low range compared to high powered rifles, which

### Table 9. Parental Status of Male Hunters by Hunting Activity of Children and Species Pursued: 2001
*(Population 16 Years of Age and Older. Numbers in Thousands)*

| | All Male Hunters | Percent of All Hunters | Males without Children | Percent | Males with Children who Did Not Hunt | Percent | Males with Children who Hunted | Percent |
|---|---|---|---|---|---|---|---|---|
| **Total, All Hunters** | 11,845 | 100% | 7,871 | 100% | 2,439 | 100% | 1,535 | 100% |
| **Big Game** | 9,923 | 84% | 6,572 | 84% | 2,000 | 82% | 1,351 | 88% |
| Deer | 9,371 | 79% | 6,210 | 79% | 1,882 | 77% | 1,280 | 83% |
| Elk | 831 | 7% | 539 | 7% | 168 | 7% | 123 | 8% |
| Bear | 340 | 3% | 211 | 3% | 79 | 3% | 50 | 3% |
| Turkey | 2,330 | 20% | 1,560 | 20% | 352 | 14% | 417 | 27% |
| Moose | 58 | (Z) | 38 | (Z) | *11 | (Z) | *9 | *1% |
| Other Big Game | 449 | 4% | 304 | 4% | 46 | 2% | 99 | 6% |
| **Small Game** | 5,114 | 43% | 3,398 | 43% | 930 | 38% | 786 | 51% |
| Rabbit | 1,968 | 17% | 1,301 | 17% | 328 | 13% | 339 | 22% |
| Quail | 938 | 8% | 610 | 8% | 208 | 9% | 119 | 8% |
| Grouse | 949 | 8% | 626 | 8% | 149 | 6% | 174 | 11% |
| Squirrel | 1,998 | 17% | 1,369 | 17% | 268 | 11% | 360 | 23% |
| Pheasant | 1,630 | 14% | 1,025 | 13% | 348 | 14% | 257 | 17% |
| Other Small Game | 481 | 4% | 336 | 4% | 96 | 4% | *49 | *3% |
| **Migratory Bird** | 2,815 | 24% | 1,779 | 23% | 575 | 24% | 461 | 30% |
| Geese | 970 | 8% | 617 | 8% | 197 | 8% | 156 | 10% |
| Duck | 1,517 | 13% | 1,031 | 13% | 266 | 11% | 220 | 14% |
| Dove | 1,362 | 11% | 820 | 10% | 281 | 12% | 261 | 17% |
| Other Migratory Bird | 206 | 2% | 126 | 2% | *39 | *2% | *41 | *3% |
| **Other Animals** | 1,005 | 8% | 678 | 9% | 138 | 6% | 189 | 12% |

*Estimate based on small sample size.
(Z) indicates less than 0.5%

reduces the risk associated with errant shots that are probably made more often by children than adults. Another factor that favors small game and migratory birds as introductory species is greater opportunities to shoot these firearms. There are more chances to take animals in these forms of hunting, which may be more interesting and instructive to children.

Small game hunting has experienced a decade-long decline in participation. Total participation in small game hunting was 7.6 million in 1991, fell to 6.9 million in 1996, and then fell again to 5.4 million in 2001. The decline in small game hunting comprised the largest portion of the decline in all hunting from 14.1 million participants in 1991 to 13.0 million participants in 2001. Given the importance of small game as an introductory species, this trend could indicate a declining exposure of children to hunting.

The 1996 and 2001 *FHWARs* can be used to ascertain who experienced the sharpest decline in small game hunting: male hunters without children, those with children who did not hunt, or those with children who hunted. Chart 11 presents the percentage decline in small game participants from 1996 to 2001. Small game hunting had the sharpest decline among those males with children who did not hunt, and it declined the least among males with children who hunted.

The relatively slight decline among males with children who hunted is likely another indicator of the importance of small game as introductory species. It could be that factors related to hunting quality or availability had a negative impact on the number of small game hunters from 1996 to 2001. Perhaps access to small game hunting areas diminished or there were fewer animals or less desirable animals to pursue. A number of factors could have contributed to the decline in small game hunting. However, whatever factors contributed to the overall decline, apparently they had less impact on hunters for whom small game hunting is particularly important: males with children who participated.

*Regression Analysis*
Table 9 clearly indicates that male hunters with children who hunted had relativity high concentrations in species in which small caliber rifles or shotguns are used. However, the descriptive statistics in Table 9 don't tell the whole

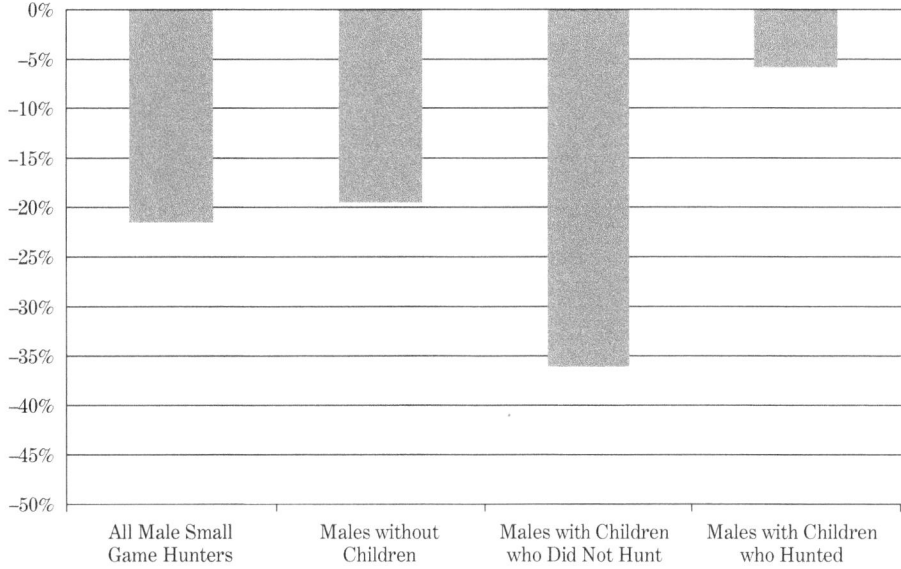

**Chart 11. Percent Decline in the Number of Male Small Game Hunters from 1996 to 2001**

story. They do not reveal the independent effect each characteristic has on the likelihood of having children who hunted, nor do they permit an assessment of whether the apparent relationship occurred by chance. Besides the species pursued, other characteristics also appear to have a relationship with the likelihood of having children who hunted. For example, male hunters who resided in rural areas were more likely to have children who hunted than those who resided in urban areas.

By using regression analysis the independent effect of each characteristic on the likelihood of having children who hunted can be isolated and the significance of the relationship can be determined. Additionally, regression permits assessment of whether the correlations of the different variables with likelihood of having children who hunted are significant. In other words it permits an assessment of the probability that the relationship occurred by chance.

Logit regression is appropriate for situations where the dependent variable has two possible values, which is the case here: some male hunters had children who hunted and others had children who did not hunt. Hence, the only hunters included in the regression are those with children present in the household. Results of the regression analysis are summarized here. Details are shown in Appendix B.

When controlling for other factors that also have a relationship with likelihood of having children who hunted, several small game species have a significant impact on participation. The likelihood a male hunter had a child that hunted increases significantly if the male hunter pursued squirrel or grouse. The increase is particularly high if the male parent pursued squirrel. These results support the notion that squirrel and grouse often serve as introductory species in hunting.

One small game species, quail, actually has a significant negative impact on the likelihood of male parents having children who hunted. A complete explanation for why male parents who hunted quail would be less likely to have a child at home who hunted remains elusive. One explanation may be that quail hunting often occurs in club settings or other settings where one is likely to go hunting with several friends. In such a setting it may not be appropriate to bring along novice hunters who lack a high degree of gun proficiency and awareness of the activities of other hunters. Alternatively, male hunters who lack companionship of their children may be more likely to participate in the 'buddy' hunting nature of quail hunting.

There are a couple of non-small game species associated with a significant increase in the likelihood of having children who participated. Male parents who pursued turkey and dove were also more likely to have a child who hunted. The result for turkey hunting is particularly encouraging because it expanded through the nineties. In 1991 there were 1.2 million turkey hunters who pursued turkey 13.5 million days. This increased to 2.5 million hunters and 23.2 million days by 2001. Provided turkey is a viable introductory species, these increases could indicate a rising genre of hunting in which recruiting is likely on the rise. Perhaps turkey hunting could counter the decline in recruits resulting from contraction in small game hunting.

Besides species hunted, other factors also have significant relationships with the likelihood of male hunters having children who hunted. The most important[17] is the number of days the male parent hunts. Not surprising, the higher number of days a male parent hunted, the higher the likelihood of having a child who hunted.

Several factors related to the availability of hunting opportunities significantly increased the likelihood of having children who hunted. Male parents who hunted on private land were significantly more likely to have children who hunted than those who only hunted on public land. All other things equal, those constrained to hunt only on public land may find taking children along more difficult or risky than those who have access to private land.

Higher incomes are also associated with a significantly higher increase in likelihood of having children who hunted. All other things equal, higher incomes could increase the number of opportunities in which hunters could afford to take their children along.

Residents of rural areas are significantly more likely to have children who participated than residents of urban areas with one million people or more. Interestingly, there is no statistically significant difference between residents of rural areas and urban areas of less than one million people.

Hispanic male parents who hunted had a lower likelihood of having children who hunted than Non-Hispanics. Interestingly, the race of hunters was not significant.

Lastly, male parents who hunted on leased land were significantly less likely to have children who hunted than those who hunted on land that was not leased. Hunting leases are often made by a group of individuals with a landowner. The group often comprises friends or colleagues so, as in the case of quail hunters, leased land may not be an appropriate place for the tutelage of an inexperienced hunter. Another possible explanation, however, is that those who lease land with friends and colleagues may lack the company of others from within the family.

---

[17] In this context "most important" means that it explains the largest amount of variation in likelihood of having children who hunt.

# Retention

Having analyzed information available from the *FHWAR* concerning recruitment, it is now time to shift gears and see what information it contains about retention of individuals in fishing and hunting. As discussed above, individuals are no longer considered active anglers or hunters if they did not participate in the activity for three years prior to the *detail* survey years 1991, 1996, 2001, or 2006. Thus, individuals who did participate in one of the three years prior to these survey years are considered active anglers or hunters. For example, for the 2001 *FHWAR*, an individual is considered a dropout from fishing if she had fished at some point in her life but did not participate in 2000, 1999, or 1998.

In this section "remained active" refers to participation in fishing or hunting in one of the three years prior to a survey. The "retention rate" is the percent of individuals who have participated in fishing or hunting at some point and have remained active in the respective activity.

## Age of Dropouts

Information from the *FHWAR* is useful in discerning the percent of the population who previously participated in fishing and hunting and have remained active in at least one of three years prior to the survey year. These percentages can be calculated and graphed for individuals of different ages. These graphs serve as "dropout curves" that indicate ages where quitting is particularly acute. The dropout curves for fishing and hunting from the 1991 and 2006 *FHWARs* are displayed in Charts 12 and 13.

Fishing retention declines rapidly through the teenage years, levels out from the early twenties through the early forties, declines at a fairly constant rate from the early forties until the early sixties, and declines rapidly beyond the age of 68. From the early forties until 61, the retention rate, which is the percent active within the three prior years, decreases about three percent a year.

**Chart 12. Percent of Anglers Still Active\* by Age: 1990 and 2005**

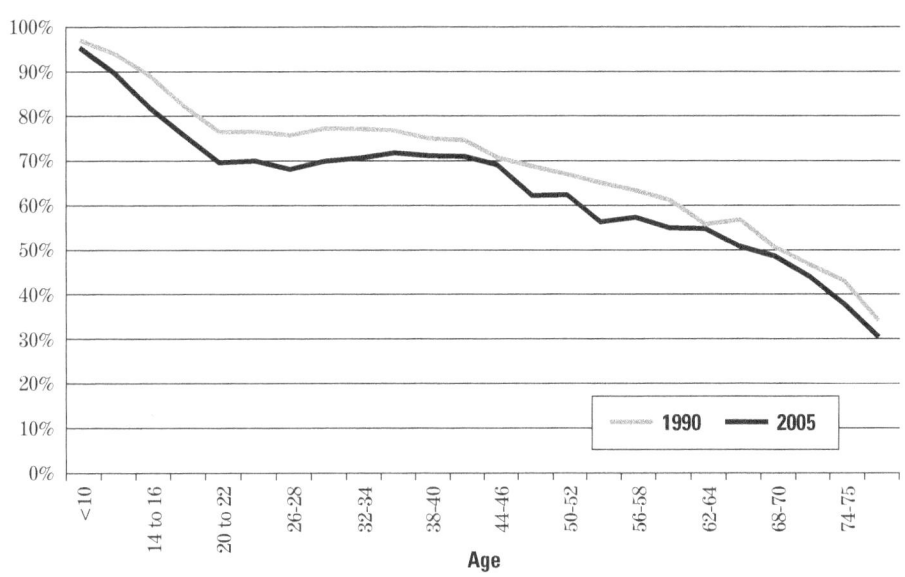

\* *Individuals who participated in one of the three years prior to the 1991 (1990, 1989, 1988) and 2006 (2005, 2004, 2003) surveys.*

**Chart 13. Percent of Hunters Still Active\* by Age: 1990 and 2005**

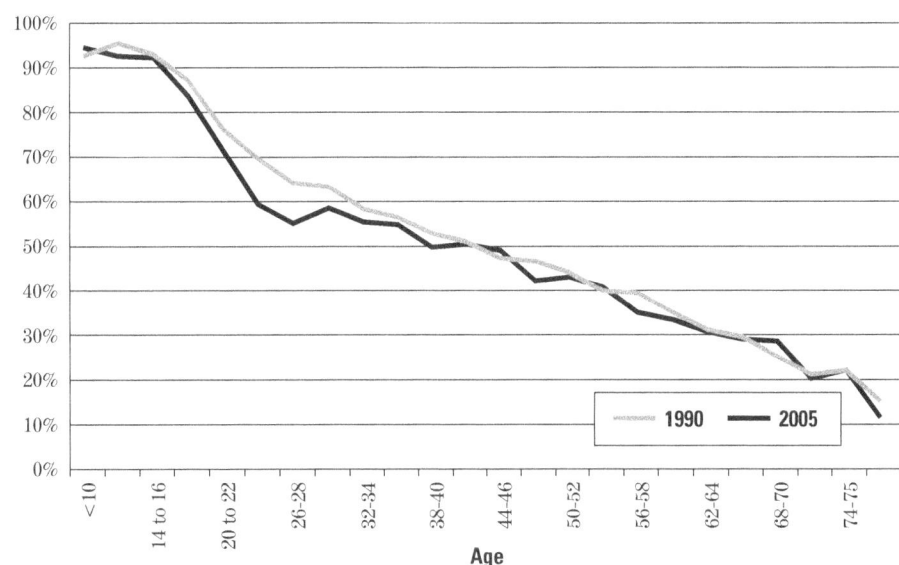

\* *Individuals who participated in one of the three years prior to the 1991 (1990, 1989, 1988) and 2006 (2005, 2004, 2003) surveys.*

Hunting retention also decreases rapidly through the teenage years; but, unlike fishing, after the age of 25 the retention rate for hunting declines rather steadily until 75 years of age. In both the 1990 and 2005 Surveys, there was no level period for hunting retention. Apparently, individuals quit participating at a rather steady progression.

From 1990 to 2005, the fishing retention rate decreased for all age individuals, which is indicated by the line for 2005 in Chart 12 lying below that for 1990. For hunting, the retention rate declined for individuals under 35 years of age, but for those 35 and over the retention rate for hunting is about the same.

### Characteristics of Dropouts

Tables 10-13 present the retention rate by socioeconomic characteristics. Incorporating the socioeconomic information yields a better understanding of the "types" of individuals who are more likely to quit fishing. The discussion here focuses on changes in the retention rate for individuals of any age, but tables A-3 and A-4 in the appendix can be used to analyze changes among different age cohorts.

In 2005 the retention rate for fishing among different geographic regions reveals that anglers in the West North Central region had the highest retention rate at 63%[18]. This is not surprising since it is the region that historically has the highest participation rate in fishing. The retention rate was lowest in the Pacific region[19], which indicates that individuals who were exposed to fishing at some point were more likely to quit fishing in the Pacific region than in other regions of the U.S. Also, perhaps not surprising, females had a lower retention rate than males, and urban residents had a lower retention rate than rural residents. Among females of any age, 49% remained active in 2005, which compares to 62% of males. 54% of urban residents remained active compared to 66% of rural residents.

---

[18]The retention rate is significantly higher (90% level) in the West North Central than all other regions except East and West South Central.

[19]The retention rate is significantly lower (90% level) in the Pacific than all other regions.

## Table 10. Fishing Retention Rates by Selected Characteristics: 1990, 1995, 2000, and 2005
*(Population 16 Years of Age and Older)*

|  | 2005 | 2000 | 1995 | 1990 | Difference* 1990-2005 | Percent Change 1990-2005 |
|---|---|---|---|---|---|---|
| **U.S. Total** | 57% | 60% | 61% | 65% | –8% | –13% |
| **Geographic Regions** | | | | | | |
| New England | 54% | 56% | 59% | 62% | –8% | –13% |
| Middle Atlantic | 54% | 57% | 59% | 62% | –9% | –14% |
| East North Central | 60% | 60% | 63% | 65% | –5% | –7% |
| West North Central | 63% | 66% | 66% | 67% | –3% | –5% |
| South Atlantic | 59% | 63% | 62% | 69% | –10% | –14% |
| East South Central | 61% | 65% | 65% | 70% | –9% | –13% |
| West South Central | 61% | 61% | 64% | 70% | –9% | –13% |
| Mountain | 53% | 58% | 60% | 64% | –11% | –17% |
| Pacific | 49% | 52% | 53% | 60% | –11% | –19% |
| **Gender** | | | | | | |
| Male | 62% | 65% | 67% | 71% | –9% | –12% |
| Female | 49% | 51% | 52% | 57% | –8% | –14% |
| **Ethnicity** | | | | | | |
| Non-Hispanic | 57% | 59% | 61% | 65% | –8% | –12% |
| Hispanic | 58% | 66% | 65% | 70% | –12% | –17% |
| **Race** | | | | | | |
| White | 58% | 60% | 61% | 66% | –8% | –12% |
| Black | 52% | 53% | 57% | 61% | –9% | –15% |
| Other | 49% | 58% | 62% | 67% | –18% | –27% |
| **Population Density** | | | | | | |
| Urban Area | 54% | 56% | 58% | 62% | –9% | –14% |
| Rural Area | 66% | 67% | 67% | 72% | –6% | –9% |

*All differences significant at 90% level.

Note: Retention rates for fishing are calculated as the percent who have ever participated in fishing who were active in at least one of the three years prior to the 1991 (1990, 1989, 1988) or 2006 (2005, 2004, 2003) Surveys. The difference is the retention rate in 2005 minus the retention rate in 1990, so for all the U.S. the difference in retention in hunting is given by 57%–65%, which equals –8%. The percent change in the retention rate is a measure of relative change that makes the difference a percent of the initial rate in 1990. The percent change for all the U.S. from fishing is given by the expression $((0.571-0.653)\div0.653)\times100$, which equals –13%.

## Table 11. Fishing Retention Rates by Selected Characteristics: 1995, 2000, and 2005
*(Population 16 Years of Age and Older)*

|  | 2005 | 2000 | 1995 | Difference 1995-2005 | Percent Change 1995-2005 |
|---|---|---|---|---|---|
| **U.S. Total** | 57% | 60% | 61% | –4% | –6% |
| **Annual Household Income (2005 dollars)** | | | | | |
| Under $25,000 | 51% | NA | 53% | –2% | –4% |
| $25,000-$39,999 | 56% | NA | 61% | –6% | –9% |
| $40,000-$99,999 | 62% | NA | 65% | –3% | –5% |
| $100,000 or More | 62% | NA | 64% | –2% | –3% |
| **Metropolitan Statistical Area** | | | | | |
| Inside MSA in Central City | 49% | 53% | 55% | –6% | –11% |
| Inside MSA not in Central City | 58% | 60% | 61% | –3% | –4% |
| Outside MSA | 64% | 65% | 68% | –4% | –5% |

*\*All differences significant at 90% level except the following: those with incomes Under $25,000 and $100,000 or More.*
*NA= Not Available*
*Note: Retention rates for fishing are calculated as the percent who have ever participated in fishing who were active in at least one of the three years prior to the 1996 (1995, 1994, 1993) or 2006 (2005, 2004, 2003) Surveys. The **difference** is the retention rate in 2005 minus the retention rate in 1996, so for all the U.S. the difference in retention in hunting is given by 57%– 61%, which equals –4%. The **percent change** in the retention rate is a measure of relative change that makes the difference a percent of the initial rate in 1990. The percent change for all the U.S. from fishing is given by the expression ((0.571–0.610)÷0.610)×100, which equals –6%.*

Tables 10 and 11 show some results that are probably less expected, such as those for ethnicity and income. The fishing retention rate is relatively similar for all income levels, but it is highest for those with incomes of $40,000 or more and lowest for those with incomes under $25,000. This could indicate that costs associated with fishing are a deterrent to participation among those in the lowest income strata. It is important to note that the costs associated with fishing are not limited to equipment, licenses, fuel, etc. Costs also include those associated with spending time in leisure activities such as fishing and not working.

It is noteworthy that Hispanics don't drop out at a faster rate than Non-Hispanics. In 2005 the retention rate was about the same for Hispanics and Non-Hispanics at 58% and 57% respectively. In 2000 the retention rate was higher for Hispanics at 66%, which compares to 59% for Non-Hispanics[20]. These data support the conclusion that lower participation rates among Hispanics are more likely the result of lower recruitment rates.

[20] The retention rate of Hispanics is significantly higher at 95% level than Non-Hispanics.

Tables 12 and 13 present hunting retention rates. Among different geographic regions, the West North Central had the highest retention[21]. Like fishing, the participation rate in the West North Central is also the highest for hunting. Also similar to fishing, the Pacific region had the lowest hunting retention rate. However, the difference between the retention rates among the Pacific and other regions is greater for hunting than for fishing. Also not surprising, given their lower participation rates, females had a lower retention rate than males.

Like anglers, hunters with incomes under $25,000 had the lowest retention rate. The highest retention occurs among individuals with incomes of $40,000-$99,999.

Residents of urban areas had lower retention rates than those in rural areas. This suggests that the higher participation rate for hunting in rural areas is not only due to higher recruitment but also to higher retention.

## Trend in Retention

The trend in fishing and hunting retention can be analyzed in detail by examining changes in the retention rate over time and incorporating socioeconomic information. Just as in the analysis of recruitment, the concept of a *percent change* in the retention rate is also useful in discerning trends.

The difference in the retention rates from 1990 to 2000 is also useful. The differences can be used to approximate, with some qualifications, the total number of additional active anglers and hunters there would have been in 2000 if the retention rate had remained unchanged from 1990 to 2000. Generally, the *screen* data is considered more reliable for percentage estimates than for participation levels because of the potential for bias associated with recall of more than one year of activity, which is required for screen interviews but not for detail interviews. Consequently, participation numbers should be viewed as ballpark estimates only; additional research would be required to refine these approximations.

---

[21] The retention rate in the West North Central Region is significantly higher at 95% level than all but three other regions: Middle Atlantic, East North Central, and West South Central.

### Table 12. Hunting Retention Rates by Selected Characteristics: 1990, 1995, 2000, and 2005
*(Population 16 Years of Age and Older)*

| | 2005 | 2000 | 1995 | 1990 | Difference*<br>1990-2005 | Percent<br>Change<br>1990-2005 |
|---|---|---|---|---|---|---|
| **U.S. Total** | 43% | 43% | 45% | 49% | –7% | –14% |
| **Geographic Regions** | | | | | | |
| New England | 38% | 41% | 45% | 46% | –8% | –18% |
| Middle Atlantic | 47% | 49% | 50% | 54% | –7% | –13% |
| East North Central | 47% | 47% | 49% | 50% | –3% | –7% |
| West North Central | 50% | 51% | 53% | 52% | –2% | –3% |
| South Atlantic | 40% | 40% | 40% | 48% | –8% | –17% |
| East South Central | 46% | 48% | 51% | 55% | –9% | –17% |
| West South Central | 47% | 46% | 49% | 54% | –7% | –13% |
| Mountain | 36% | 42% | 45% | 50% | –14% | –28% |
| Pacific | 27% | 28% | 33% | 36% | –9% | –25% |
| **Gender** | | | | | | |
| Male | 44% | 46% | 48% | 51% | –7% | –14% |
| Female | 33% | 32% | 33% | 38% | –5% | –14% |
| **Ethnicity** | | | | | | |
| Non-Hispanic | 42% | 43% | 45% | 49% | –7% | –14% |
| Hispanic | 45% | 43% | 45% | 53% | –8% | –15% |
| **Race** | | | | | | |
| White | 43% | 44% | 46% | 50% | –7% | –13% |
| Non-White | 33% | 33% | 39% | 41% | –8% | –19% |
| **Population Density** | | | | | | |
| Urban Area | 35% | 36% | 39% | 43% | –8% | –18% |
| Rural Area | 53% | 53% | 54% | 59% | –5% | –9% |

*All differences significant at 90% level except the following: West North Central Geographic Region.
Note: Retention rates for hunting are calculated as the percent who have ever participated in fishing who were active in at least one of the three years prior to the 1991 (1990, 1989, 1988) or 2006 (2005, 2004, 2003) Surveys. The difference is the retention rate in 2005 minus the retention rate in 1990, so for all the U.S. the difference in retention in hunting is given by 43%–49%, which equals –7%. The percent change in the retention rate is a measure of relative change that makes the difference a percent of the initial rate in 1990. The percent change for all the U.S. from fishing is given by the expression ((0.425–0.493)÷0.493)×100, which equals –14%.

**Table 13. Hunting Retention Rates by Selected Characteristics: 1995, 2000, and 2005**
*(Population 16 Years of Age and Older)*

| | 2005 | 2000 | 1995 | Difference 1995-2005 | Percent Change 1995-2005 |
|---|---|---|---|---|---|
| **U.S. Total** | 43% | 43% | 45% | –3% | –6% |
| **Annual Household Income (2005 dollars)** | | | | | |
| Under $25,000 | 31% | NA | 34% | –3% | –9% |
| $25,000-$39,999 | 41% | NA | 47% | –7% | –14% |
| $40,000-$99,999 | 48% | NA | 49% | –1% | –3% |
| $100,000 or More | 47% | NA | 47% | (Z) | (Z) |
| **Metropolitan Statistical Area** | | | | | |
| Inside MSA in Central City | 32% | 35% | 37% | –6% | –15% |
| Inside MSA not in Central City | 42% | 41% | 43% | –1% | –2% |
| Outside MSA | 51% | 52% | 55% | –4% | –7% |

*All differences Significant at 90% level of significance except the following: Incomes of Under 25,000, $40,000-$99,999, $100,000 or more, and Inside MSA Not in Central City.*
*NA = Not Available*
*(Z) = less than 0.5%.*
*Note: Retention rates for hunting are calculated as the percent who have ever participated in fishing who were active in at least one of the three years prior to the 1996 (1995, 1994, 1993) or 2006 (2005, 2004, 2003) Surveys. The difference is the retention rate in 2005 minus the retention rate in 1995, so for all the U.S. the difference in retention in hunting is given by 43%–45%, which equals –6%. The percent change in the retention rate is a measure of relative change that makes the difference a percent of the initial rate in 1990. The percent change for all the U.S. from fishing is given by the expression ((0.425–0.493)÷0.454)×100, which equals –6%.*

For fishing, Table 10 indicates that the retention rate for individuals 16 years and older in 2005 was 8% lower than in 1990. Data from the *screen* survey indicates that in 2005, 102 million individuals 16 and over had ever participated in fishing. Of this 102 million, 58 million are considered active anglers because they participated from 2003-2005. If 8% more of those who had ever participated remained active sometime from 2003-2005, then the number of active anglers in 2005 could have been as high as 66 million. If the retention rate for hunting had not decreased, the number of individuals considered active hunters could have been 21.5 million instead of 18.5 million. This does not mean that 66 million people will fish or 21.5 million will hunt in the *detail phase* survey year of 2006, since persons considered active for purposes of this report were only required to participate in one of the three prior years. The number of people considered active anglers and hunters will, realistically, always be higher than the number who actually hunt or fish in a single specific year.

The *percent changes* in retention rates for fishing and hunting that occurred from 1990 to 2000 and 1995 to 2005 are shown in Tables 10-13. These *percent changes* reveal several interesting details about which groups of individuals have experienced the least decrease in fishing and hunting retention.

Those with higher incomes experienced the least decrease in fishing retention from 1995 to 2005. The *percent changes* indicate that the decline in retention was slowest among those with incomes of $100,000 or more. The decline in retention among those with incomes of $25,000-$39,999 was about three times greater than those with incomes of $100,000 or more. These results support a conclusion that costs associated with fishing were likely a contributor to reduced fishing participation.

There are other interesting results with respect to fishing retention. Fishing retention declined the most in the Mountain and Pacific regions. The retention rate declined more among residents of urban areas than rural areas.

Lastly, the retention decline among central city MSA residents was twice that of the both MSA residents who don't live in a central city and those who live outside MSAs (Table 11).

For hunting, those with lower incomes experienced the largest decrease in the retention rate, and similar to the change in the initiation rate discussed above, $40,000 appears to be a threshold. The retention rate for individuals with incomes under $25,000 decreased from 34% in 1995 to 31% in 2005. This represents a *percent change* in the retention rate of –9%. Additionally, the *percent change* for those with incomes of $25,000-$39,999 was –14%. The change in the hunting retention rate among those with incomes of $40,000 or more was appreciably less. For those with incomes of $100,000 there was no decline in the retention rate, and the slight decline for those with incomes of $40,000-$99,999 is not statistically significant. Data for both hunting recruitment and retention suggest that cost considerations may well have constrained hunting participation from 1995 to 2005.

The decrease in hunting retention rates by geographic regions was sharpest in the Mountain and Pacific states. As with fishing, the West North Central region experienced the smallest decrease in retention. In fact, with a *percent change* of only –3%, one could say that retention was virtually identical in 1990 and 2005. The *percent change* in the retention rate in the East North Central region was also half the national average of –14%.

The sizable difference between the East and West North Central regions and the rest of the country spurs additional questions. Were there regulatory practices in these two regions that made a difference in retaining hunters? Was the difference due to greater accessibility of quality hunting areas? Was the difference related to the species pursued with greater frequency in these areas?

## Reasons for Quitting

*Inactive Anglers and Hunters in 2001*
As discussed above, the purpose of the *screen phase* of the *FHWAR* is to identify individuals who are likely to participate in fishing or hunting during the survey year. These sample persons are then administered the *detail phase* questions about their activities and expenditures at three different times during the survey year.

Since many sample persons were selected on the basis of their "likelihood" of participating, some people selected for *detail* interviews do not end up hunting, fishing, or both during the survey year. In the last round of *detail* interviews in the 2001 survey, these individuals were asked why they did not participate. This section analyzes their answers to better understand why individuals stop participating.

The universe of individuals addressed in this section is quite different from that analyzed in the "Age of Dropouts," "Characteristics of Dropouts," and "Trend in Retention" sections for the following reasons. First, those sections address all individuals in the U.S. because a random sample of all households answered the *screen phase* questions. However, the *detail phase* only includes people who were considered likely anglers or hunters, so we only have answers to these questions for this segment of the U.S. population.

Second, some individuals were selected on the basis of their expected fishing activity alone without consideration of whether they would participate in hunting. Consequently, a substantial portion of expected anglers queried why they did not participate in hunting reported something similar to "not a hunter and did not intend to go." A similar story is true for hunting. In an attempt to eliminate those who were not deemed viable participants, sample persons who reported "not an angler and did not intend to go fishing" are eliminated from the analysis of why individuals did not go fishing. Those who are analyzed are referred to as "probable" anglers in Tables 14 and 16. Alternatively, sample persons who reported that they were not hunters and did not intend to go hunting are eliminated from the analysis of why individuals did not go hunting. Those who are analyzed are referred to as "probable" hunters in Tables 15 and 17. This approach allows us to focus on reasons reported by viable or likely participants.

### Table 14. Reasons Probable Anglers Did Not Fish: 2001
*(Population 16 Years of Age and Older Administered Detail Interview)*

| | Years Inactive | |
| --- | --- | --- |
| | *3 or Less* | *More than 3* |
| Not Enough Time | 49% | 42% |
| Family or Work | 37% | 36% |
| School | 6% | 5% |
| Not Enough Money/Cost Too Much | 5% | 3% |
| Health/Disability | 10% | 14% |
| No One to Fish With | 4% | 6% |
| Place Related | 2% | 1% |
| Regulation Related | (Z) | ** |
| Other | 14% | 15% |

*\*\*Sample size too small to report data reliably.*
*(Z) indicates less than 0.5%.*
*Note: **Probable Anglers** represent a segment of the population that were selected for the detailed interview phase and did not report that they were not anglers.*
*Note: **Place Related** includes responses citing Not Enough Places/Access to Places, Places Too Crowded, Don't Know Where to Go, and Not Enough Fish. **Regulation Related** includes responses citing Catch Limits Too Restrictive and Length of Fishing Season Too Restrictive.*

In Tables 14 and 15 individuals 16 years of age and older who did not participate are grouped into two categories depending on how many years they were inactive: inactive for three years or less and inactive for more than three years. The distinction is intended to distinguish between those who are probably more and those probably less likely to return to the activities and is consistent with the prior discussion of retention.

Table 14 shows that the reasons reported for not fishing in 2001 were similar for sample persons who were inactive three years or less and those inactive more than three years. Those inactive three years or less reported not enough time at a higher rate than those inactive more than three years, 49% compared to 42%. Those inactive three years or less had a lower percentage reporting health/disability than those inactive more than three years, 10% compared to 14%.

Among probable hunters inactive three years or less and inactive more than three years, response frequencies were notably different for a few of the cited reasons (Table 15). Those inactive for longer said family or work obligations less often, 38% compared to 46%. Those inactive for longer cited health/disability as a reason more often, 22% compared to 14%. At 8% Cost is apparently a greater issue for those who have been inactive for three years or less. School is a greater

issue among those inactive for a shorter period of time, 8% compared to 3%.

*Reasons for Quitting by Socioeconomic Characteristics*
A question of interest is whether the reasons reported for not fishing or hunting differ among individuals with different socioeconomic characteristics. For example, among those with higher incomes, one would expect that citing "not enough money/cost too much" would be less common given their additional available income to pursue hunting or fishing. Tables 16 and 17 show the percentage of individuals with different socioeconomic characteristics citing their reasons for not fishing and hunting. To maximize the number of observations available for the different cells, the distinction between inactive three years or less and inactive more than three years is not repeated. Otherwise, many of the cells would not have enough observations to report the data reliably.

Table 16 presents reasons why individuals did not participate in fishing. The regions of the country are grouped differently than in the prior sections of the report in an effort to pool observations. The regions are composed as follows: New England and Middle Atlantic comprise the North East; East and West North Central comprise the Midwest; East and West South Central along with South Atlantic comprise the

## Table 15. Reasons Probable Hunters Did Not Hunt: 2001
*(Population 16 Years of Age and Older Administered Detail Interview)*

| | Years Inactive | |
|---|---|---|
| | *3 or Less* | *More than 3* |
| Not Enough Time | 44% | 43% |
| Family or Work | 46% | 38% |
| School | 8% | 3% |
| Not Enough Money/Cost Too Much | 8% | 5% |
| Health/Disability | 14% | 22% |
| No One to Hunt With | 3% | 4% |
| Place Related | 2% | 3% |
| Regulation Related | 2% | (Z) |
| Other | 7% | 8% |

*(Z) indicates less than 0.5%.*
*Note: **Probable Hunters** represent a segment of the population that were selected for the detailed interview phase and did not report that they were not hunters.*
*Note: **Place Related** includes responses citing Not Enough Places/Access to Places, Places Too Crowded, Don't Know Where to Go, and Not Enough Game. **Regulation Related** includes responses citing Bag Limits Too Restrictive, Length of Hunting Season Too Restrictive, Did Not Draw License in Lottery.*

South; Mountain and Pacific comprise the West. There is not much variation in reported reasons for not fishing among different geographic regions.

The reasons reported by gender were also quite similar with the only notable difference being that a higher percentage of males reported not enough time as a reason.

The results for Non-Hispanics versus Hispanics are interesting because of the rapid growth in the Hispanic population in recent years and likely continued growth in the near future. Increased participation by Hispanics will likely be necessary to keep the overall participation rate in fishing near its current level, especially in certain regions of the US. Hispanics were more likely to report not enough time, family or work, and cost as reasons for not participating. 4% of Non-Hispanics reported cost as a reason for not participating, compared to 10% of Hispanics. Hispanics were less likely to report health/disability as a reason.

The results by income are also interesting. Those with household incomes of $40,000 or more were more likely to report not enough time and family or work as reasons, while those with incomes under $40,000 were more likely to report cost and health/disability as reasons. Those with incomes less than

$40,000 cited cost as a reason at more than twice the rate of those with incomes of $40,000 or more: 7% compared to 3%. 19% of those with incomes under $40,000 cited health/disability, which is more than three times the percent of those with more income at 6%. The higher percent reporting health/disability among those with incomes of less than $40,000 is undoubtedly related to the large number of elderly in this category.

Not surprisingly, the results by age reveal that school is the primary reason for those 16-24 years old, and health/disability is the primary reason for those 65 and over. For the primary child-rearing years of 25-54, not enough time was the primary reason cited. Interestingly, for those years in which one is most likely to have adolescent children, 34-54, no one to fish with was less of a concern than it was for other age groups.

Other noteworthy results include the following. Non-Whites were more likely to report cost and disability as reasons for not fishing. Those residing in urban areas and those residing in the central cities of MSAs were slightly more likely to report cost as a reason, while those residing in rural areas and those outside MSAs were more likely to report health/disability. Those with less than four years of college were more likely to report school, cost, and health/disability as reasons.

The results for probable hunters are presented in Table 17. Probable hunters in most of the regions were fairly similar in their responses, but those in the West do appear to distinguish themselves. They were less likely to say not enough time and health/disability and were more likely to cite cost and no one to hunt with. The reasons reported by gender were also quite similar with the only notable difference being that a higher percentage of males reported not enough time as a reason.

Other noteworthy results for hunting include the following. Hispanics were more likely than Non-Hispanics to report not enough time and family or work and less likely to report health/disability. Whites were less likely to report not enough time. Those residing in urban areas and central cities of MSAs were more likely to cite cost, while those residing in rural areas and outside MSAs were more likely to cite health/disability. Those with less than four years of college cited school, cost, and health/disability at greater rates than those with four years of college or more.

For hunting the results by age and income are similar to those for fishing. School is cited as a reason by 32% of those 16-24, which is substantially higher than those in other age groups. Health/disability is cited by 65% of those 65 and over. Those with incomes of $40,000 or more were more likely to report not enough time and family or work. Those with incomes under $40,000 were more likely to report cost and health/disability. Those with incomes under $40,000 cited cost at more than twice the rate and health/disability at more than three times the rate as those with incomes of $40,000 or more.

## Table 16. Why Quit?—Probable Anglers Not Active in 2001 by Socioeconomic Characteristics
*(Population 16 Years of Age and Older )*

| | Not Enough Time | Family or Work | School | Cost | Health/ Disability | No One to Fish With | Place Related | Regulation Related | Other |
|---|---|---|---|---|---|---|---|---|---|
| **U.S. Total** | 47% | 37% | 6% | 4% | 11% | 4% | 2% | (z) | 14% |
| **Geographic Regions** | | | | | | | | | |
| North East | 46% | 34% | 4% | 2% | 11% | 3% | 2% | 1% | 19% |
| Midwest | 50% | 35% | 5% | 3% | 10% | 4% | 1% | ** | 16% |
| South | 45% | 39% | 6% | 5% | 13% | 4% | 2% | ** | 11% |
| West | 49% | 38% | 6% | 6% | 9% | 5% | 3% | 1% | 15% |
| **Gender** | | | | | | | | | |
| Male | 50% | 37% | 6% | 5% | 11% | 4% | 2% | (z) | 12% |
| Female | 44% | 37% | 4% | 4% | 11% | 5% | 2% | 1% | 17% |
| **Ethnicity** | | | | | | | | | |
| Non-Hispanic | 47% | 37% | 5% | 4% | 11% | 4% | 2% | 0% | 14% |
| Hispanic | 56% | 41% | 7% | 10% | 5% | 5% | ** | ** | 11% |
| **Race** | | | | | | | | | |
| White | 47% | 37% | 5% | 4% | 11% | 4% | 2% | 1% | 15% |
| Non-White | 50% | 35% | 6% | 7% | 14% | 6% | 2% | ** | 10% |
| **Annual Household Income** | | | | | | | | | |
| Under $40,000 | 42% | 33% | 5% | 7% | 19% | 5% | 2% | ** | 13% |
| $40,000 or More | 51% | 40% | 6% | 3% | 6% | 3% | 2% | (z) | 15% |
| **Population Area** | | | | | | | | | |
| Urban Area | 48% | 37% | 6% | 5% | 9% | 5% | 2% | (z) | 15% |
| Rural Area | 45% | 37% | 5% | 3% | 15% | 3% | 1% | 1% | 13% |
| **Metropolitan Statistical Area** | | | | | | | | | |
| Inside MSA in Central City | 52% | 36% | 5% | 7% | 10% | 6% | 2% | ** | 13% |
| Inside MSA not in Central City | 47% | 39% | 5% | 4% | 10% | 4% | 2% | 1% | 15% |
| Outside MSA | 45% | 35% | 6% | 4% | 15% | 4% | 2% | ** | 14% |
| **Education** | | | | | | | | | |
| Less than 4 years of college | 46% | 37% | 7% | 5% | 13% | 4% | 2% | 0% | 13% |
| 4 years of college or more | 51% | 38% | 2% | 2% | 6% | 5% | 2% | 0% | 18% |
| **Age** | | | | | | | | | |
| 16-24 | 42% | 17% | 52% | ** | ** | 7% | ** | ** | 10% |
| 25 to 34 | 54% | 46% | 2% | 4% | 2% | 4% | 1% | ** | 12% |
| 35 to 44 | 52% | 42% | 1% | 5% | 5% | 3% | 2% | 1% | 14% |
| 45 to 54 | 51% | 38% | 2% | 5% | 9% | 3% | 2% | ** | 16% |
| 55 to 64 | 41% | 36% | ** | 3% | 19% | 4% | 2% | ** | 15% |
| 65+ | 23% | 15% | ** | 2% | 49% | 8% | 2% | ** | 17% |

*Estimate based on small sample size.
**Sample size too small to report data reliably.
(Z) indicates less than 0.5%.
Note: Probable Anglers represent a segment of the population that were selected for the detailed interview phase and did not report that they were not anglers.
Note: **Place Related** includes responses citing Not Enough Places/Access to Places, Places Too Crowded, Don't Know Where to Go, and Not Enough Fish.
**Regulation Related** includes responses citing Catch Limits Too Restrictive and Length of Fishing Season Too Restrictive.

## Table 17. Why Quit?—Probable Hunters Not Active in 2001 by Socioeconomic Characteristics
*(Population 16 Years of Age and Older)*

| | Not Enough Time | Family or Work | School | Cost | Health/ Disability | No One to Hunt With | Place Related | Regulation Related | Other |
|---|---|---|---|---|---|---|---|---|---|
| **U.S. Total** | 43% | 41% | 5% | 6% | 19% | 4% | 3% | 1% | 8% |
| **Geographic Regions** | | | | | | | | | |
| North East | 42% | 38% | 6% | 4% | 21% | 3% | ** | ** | 9% |
| Midwest | 47% | 41% | 4% | 5% | 20% | 3% | 2% | ** | 8% |
| South | 43% | 41% | 5% | 6% | 20% | 3% | 2% | ** | 6% |
| West | 39% | 42% | 4% | 8% | 17% | 6% | 3% | 2% | 9% |
| **Gender** | | | | | | | | | |
| Male | 44% | 40% | 5% | 7% | 19% | 4% | 3% | 1% | 8% |
| Female | 40% | 45% | 2% | 5% | 19% | 5% | ** | ** | 8% |
| **Ethnicity** | | | | | | | | | |
| Non-Hispanic | 43% | 41% | 5% | 6% | 20% | 4% | 3% | 1% | 8% |
| Hispanic | 46% | 49% | ** | ** | 12% | 0% | ** | ** | ** |
| **Race** | | | | | | | | | |
| White | 43% | 41% | 5% | 6% | 19% | 4% | 2% | 1% | 8% |
| Non-White | 50% | 39% | ** | ** | 18% | ** | ** | (Z) | 4% |
| **Annual Household Income** | | | | | | | | | |
| Under $40,000 | 34% | 33% | 5% | 10% | 31% | 4% | 3% | 1% | 9% |
| $40,000 or More | 52% | 48% | 5% | 4% | 10% | 3% | 2% | 1% | 7% |
| **Population Area** | | | | | | | | | |
| Urban Area | 44% | 42% | 4% | 7% | 16% | 5% | 3% | 1% | 9% |
| Rural Area | 43% | 39% | 5% | 5% | 24% | 2% | 2% | ** | 6% |
| **Metropolitan Statistical Area** | | | | | | | | | |
| Inside MSA in Central City | 45% | 37% | 5% | 7% | 19% | 8% | 3% | 1% | 7% |
| Inside MSA not in Central City | 44% | 43% | 4% | 6% | 16% | 3% | 3% | ** | 9% |
| Outside MSA | 42% | 40% | 5% | 6% | 24% | 3% | 2% | 2% | 6% |
| **Education** | | | | | | | | | |
| Less than 4 years of college | 40% | 40% | 5% | 7% | 22% | 4% | 3% | 1% | 8% |
| 4 years of college or more | 54% | 44% | 2% | 4% | 11% | 5% | 2% | ** | 8% |
| **Age** | | | | | | | | | |
| 16-24 | 51% | ** | 32% | ** | ** | ** | (Z) | ** | ** |
| 25 to 34 | 58% | 47% | 4% | 8% | 4% | 4% | ** | ** | 5% |
| 35 to 44 | 49% | 51% | 3% | 7% | 9% | 2% | 2% | ** | 8% |
| 45 to 54 | 50% | 45% | ** | 7% | 13% | 4% | 2% | ** | 9% |
| 55 to 64 | 36% | 40% | (Z) | 5% | 24% | 4% | 7% | ** | 10% |
| 65+ | 15% | 14% | (Z) | ** | 65% | 6% | ** | ** | 10% |

*Estimate based on small sample size.
**Sample size too small to report data reliably.
(Z) indicates less than 0.5%.
Note: *Probable Hunters* represent a segment of the population that were selected for the detailed interview phase and did not report that they were not hunters.
Note: *Place Related* includes responses citing Not Enough Places/Access to Places, Places Too Crowded, Don't Know Where to Go, and Not Enough Game.
*Regulation Related* includes responses citing Bag Limits Too Restrictive, Length of Hunting Season Too Restrictive, Did Not Draw License in Lottery.

# Summary

Throughout the decade of the nineties there was a downturn in fishing and hunting participation that concerned many natural resource managers and organizations interested in the future of these activities. Data from the *1991, 1996, 2001,* and *2006 National Survey of Fishing, Hunting, and Wildlife-Associated Recreation (FHWAR)* reveal that the declines in participation were attributable to both declining recruitment and retention.

The decline in recruitment in fishing and hunting occurred among age groups particularly important to those activities. About 10% fewer 6 to 19 year-olds living at home had ever fished in 2005 compared to those who had ever fished in 1990. The percent of 13 to 19 year olds who had ever hunted fell from 16% in 1990 to 11% in 2005.

The downward trend in recruitment was particularly sharp for some. From 1995 to 2005 the fishing initiation rate declined twice as fast for children residing in households with incomes under $40,000 than those in households with incomes of $100,000 or more. The downturn in hunting initiation among those with incomes less than $40,000 was even more pronounced. In 1995 7% of children residing in households with incomes under $25,000 had hunted at some point in their lives, but by 2005 the share had fallen to 4%. Similarly, 11% of children from households with incomes of $25,000-$39,999 had hunted in 1995, and in 2005 the share fell to 7%. Over the same time period there was virtually no decline for children in households with incomes of $40,000 or more.

Fishing and hunting recruitment was down sharply among residents of the Pacific and Mountain regions from 1990 to 2005. For hunting, New England also stands out for a particularly sharp decline. Interestingly, these regions were also the only ones that had significant downturns in fishing or hunting initiation rates from 2000 to 2005.

Data from the *FHWAR* also suggests that retention in both fishing and hunting was on the decline between 1990 and 2005. In 1990, 65% of all individuals who had ever fished in their lives remained active, which is defined as participation within the three years prior to the survey. By 2005, this percentage fell to 57%. Similarly, in 1990 49% of all individuals who had ever hunted had participated in the three years prior to the survey; by 2005 this percentage fell to 43%.

As with recruitment, certain segments of the population experienced particularly sharp decreases in retention. For fishing, the retention rate decreased sharply in the Pacific and Mountain regions and among households with incomes $25,000-$39,999. The retention rate among individuals with incomes of $25,000-$39,999 declined about twice as fast as that of individuals with household incomes of $100,000 or more.

For hunting, the retention rate was down sharply among households with incomes under $40,000. From 1995 to 2005 the retention rate among households with incomes under $25,000 and $25,000-$39,999 fell 3% and 7% respectively. This decline contrasts with virtually no decline among individuals in households with incomes of $40,000 or more.

For both fishing and hunting the declines in the retention rates were particularly sharp among residents of urban areas and central city residents of metropolitan statistical areas (MSA). This is particularly true for hunting. The hunting retention rate in urban areas declined from 43% to 35%, which compares to a decline in rural areas from 59% to 53%. In 1995 the retention rate among central city MSA residents was 37% and fell to 32% in 2005. This decline was more than twice as much as that for non-central city MSA residents and those who lived outside MSAs.

FHWAR data offer some clues that may be useful in improving overall recruitment and retention. Fishing and hunting are familial activities, with children's activities heavily influenced by the participation of parents within the household. If retention of parents in fishing and hunting can be improved, it is likely that initiation of children can also be improved.

While the survey data reveals that adolescence is an important time for recruitment, it also indicates that young and middle-aged adults also provide a substantial number of new recruits. At least a third of both first time anglers and hunters were over 20 years old. While this finding may be surprising, it is also encouraging that new recruits into hunting and fishing are not only children.

Regarding hunting, data suggest that small game hunting has a particularly important role in the initiation of children. Perhaps this suggests that programs intended to increase or improve small game hunting would encourage adults to initiate their children into hunting at greater rates than they currently do.

The cost of both fishing and hunting has been an issue to those with lower incomes. It is important to note that the costs associated with fishing and hunting are not limited to equipment, licenses, fuel, etc. Costs also include those associated with spending time in leisure activities and not working. Perhaps initiatives aimed at reducing the cost associated with fishing or hunting would be effective. However, an underlying question here is how effectively those interested in increasing hunting and fishing can affect the costs involved. Certainly many costs will be out of their control such as food, fuel, and lodging.

For both fishing and hunting the West North Central region experienced the least decrease in recruitment and retention. Perhaps there is something to be learned from this discovery. Do fish and wildlife agencies in this region have practices that could be applied elsewhere? Are fisheries and hunting areas managed any differently? Do they have different forms of outreach to promote fishing and hunting? It may just be that areas to fish and hunt are more plentiful or that there has been less urbanization, but maybe there is something that can be replicated elsewhere.

In recent years public agencies and private organizations have accelerated efforts to improve recruitment and retention in fishing and hunting. The FHWAR was not designed to ascertain the impact that these programs have had in recent years. Nevertheless, it is at least encouraging that the pace of decline in recruitment and retention that occurred throughout the Nineties did not continue over the period 2000 to 2005. For the U.S. as a whole, initiation of children in fishing and hunting remained unchanged over this period. Additionally, retention of individuals in hunting remained unchanged. Unfortunately, the most recent data indicates that the fishing retention rate did continue to decline from 2000 to 2005. However, it has not continued at the rapid pace of decline of the early Nineties. Hopefully, these findings foretell a better decade of hunting and fishing participation trends than that experienced in the Nineties.

# Appendix

# Table A-1. Percent of Sons and Daughters Residing at Home Who Have Ever Participated in Fishing by Age Cohort

| | 2005 | | | | | 2000 | | | | | 1995 | | | | | 1990 | | | | |
|---|---|---|---|---|---|---|---|---|---|---|---|---|---|---|---|---|---|---|---|---|
| | Any Age | 6-9 | 10-12 | 13-19 | 20+ | Any Age | 6-9 | 10-12 | 13-19 | 20+ | Any Age | 6-9 | 10-12 | 13-19 | 20+ | Any Age | 6-9 | 10-12 | 13-19 | 20+ |
| **U.S. Total** | 42% | 39% | 46% | 46% | 36% | 42% | 38% | 46% | 46% | 36% | 50% | 45% | 55% | 53% | 34% | 53% | 49% | 57% | 56% | 48% |
| **Geographic Regions** | | | | | | | | | | | | | | | | | | | | |
| New England | 41% | 37% | 43% | 45% | 36% | 40% | 39% | 49% | 40% | 39% | 51% | 45% | 59% | 54% | 32% | 49% | 46% | 54% | 52% | 46% |
| Middle Atlantic | 34% | 32% | 38% | 38% | 29% | 33% | 29% | 39% | 37% | 26% | 43% | 40% | 51% | 45% | 26% | 42% | 38% | 47% | 46% | 40% |
| East North Central | 47% | 47% | 52% | 49% | 40% | 45% | 40% | 50% | 51% | 35% | 50% | 47% | 58% | 52% | 35% | 57% | 55% | 61% | 61% | 51% |
| West North Central | 61% | 61% | 67% | 62% | 49% | 60% | 55% | 69% | 61% | 54% | 65% | 68% | 69% | 67% | 52% | 70% | 69% | 75% | 72% | 64% |
| South Atlantic | 41% | 38% | 47% | 44% | 35% | 40% | 39% | 43% | 43% | 33% | 49% | 44% | 53% | 52% | 33% | 49% | 44% | 52% | 53% | 46% |
| East South Central | 51% | 46% | 52% | 57% | 43% | 48% | 41% | 53% | 53% | 44% | 50% | 44% | 54% | 55% | 44% | 57% | 53% | 60% | 58% | 55% |
| West South Central | 45% | 37% | 48% | 50% | 44% | 40% | 39% | 40% | 45% | 35% | 53% | 45% | 59% | 56% | 50% | 52% | 47% | 58% | 57% | 46% |
| Mountain | 45% | 39% | 51% | 49% | 37% | 51% | 40% | 53% | 58% | 50% | 59% | 52% | 62% | 62% | 57% | 64% | 57% | 67% | 68% | 61% |
| Pacific | 32% | 27% | 33% | 38% | 28% | 37% | 33% | 39% | 43% | 31% | 43% | 35% | 47% | 47% | 42% | 49% | 44% | 52% | 51% | 49% |
| **Gender** | | | | | | | | | | | | | | | | | | | | |
| Male | 49% | 46% | 52% | 53% | 44% | 50% | 43% | 55% | 55% | 44% | 59% | 51% | 63% | 65% | 57% | 62% | 56% | 65% | 67% | 59% |
| Female | 35% | 32% | 39% | 39% | 29% | 33% | 32% | 37% | 36% | 23% | 39% | 38% | 48% | 41% | 29% | 42% | 42% | 48% | 44% | 35% |
| **Ethnicity** | | | | | | | | | | | | | | | | | | | | |
| Non-Hispanic | 46% | 44% | 51% | 50% | 39% | 45% | 41% | 50% | 49% | 36% | 53% | 48% | 59% | 56% | 46% | 55% | 52% | 60% | 59% | 50% |
| Hispanic | 22% | 17% | 25% | 24% | 22% | 24% | 21% | 25% | 28% | 21% | 26% | 21% | 25% | 28% | 30% | 31% | 26% | 33% | 34% | 32% |
| **Race** | | | | | | | | | | | | | | | | | | | | |
| White | 47% | 43% | 50% | 51% | 41% | 46% | 42% | 51% | 50% | 38% | 55% | 50% | 62% | 59% | 38% | 58% | 54% | 62% | 61% | 53% |
| Black | 23% | 21% | 25% | 25% | 19% | 20% | 14% | 21% | 24% | 18% | 23% | 23% | 22% | 22% | 18% | 27% | 19% | 27% | 32% | 27% |
| Asian | 19% | 19% | 25% | 21% | 14% | 23% | 24% | 26% | 26% | 17% | 31% | 24% | 35% | 36% | 17% | 34% | 34% | 36% | 35% | 33% |
| Other | 59% | 55% | 62% | 64% | 50% | 37% | 29% | 27% | 48% | 36% | 32% | 24% | 35% | 35% | 36% | 35% | 31% | 37% | 36% | 35% |
| **Annual Household Income (2005 dollars)** | | | | | | | | | | | | | | | | | | | | |
| Under $25,000 | 31% | 26% | 31% | 36% | 29% | NA | NA | NA | NA | NA | 34% | 34% | 38% | 35% | 30% | NA | NA | NA | NA | NA |
| $25,000-$39,999 | 36% | 32% | 40% | 38% | 33% | NA | NA | NA | NA | NA | 46% | 39% | 53% | 49% | 45% | NA | NA | NA | NA | NA |
| $40,000-$99,999 | 51% | 49% | 55% | 53% | 45% | NA | NA | NA | NA | NA | 56% | 50% | 62% | 60% | 48% | NA | NA | NA | NA | NA |
| $100,000 or More | 56% | 55% | 60% | 58% | 54% | NA | NA | NA | NA | NA | 59% | 54% | 65% | 61% | 57% | NA | NA | NA | NA | NA |
| **Metropolitan Statistical Area** | | | | | | | | | | | | | | | | | | | | |
| Inside MSA in Central City | 32% | 29% | 36% | 36% | 27% | 32% | 27% | 36% | 37% | 25% | 40% | 36% | 43% | 43% | 37% | NA | NA | NA | NA | NA |
| Inside MSA not in Central City | 44% | 42% | 48% | 48% | 39% | 43% | 40% | 47% | 46% | 36% | 51% | 45% | 58% | 53% | 46% | NA | NA | NA | NA | NA |
| Outside MSA | 52% | 47% | 54% | 56% | 46% | 53% | 48% | 56% | 58% | 44% | 59% | 57% | 66% | 61% | 52% | NA | NA | NA | NA | NA |
| **Population Density** | | | | | | | | | | | | | | | | | | | | |
| Urban Area | 38% | 35% | 42% | 41% | 32% | 38% | 35% | 42% | 42% | 31% | 45% | 41% | 50% | 48% | 42% | 48% | 44% | 52% | 52% | 45% |
| Rural Area | 56% | 51% | 57% | 60% | 51% | 52% | 48% | 56% | 56% | 46% | 60% | 56% | 68% | 62% | 51% | 63% | 60% | 67% | 66% | 56% |

NA = Not Available

# Table A-2. Percent of of Sons and Daughters Residing at Home Who Have Ever Participated in Hunting by Age Cohort

| | 2005 | | | | 2000 | | | | 1995 | | | | 1990 | | | |
|---|---|---|---|---|---|---|---|---|---|---|---|---|---|---|---|---|
| | Any Age | 6-12 | 13-19 | 20+ | Any Age | 6-12 | 13-19 | 20+ | Any Age | 6-12 | 13-19 | 20+ | Any Age | 6-12 | 13-19 | 20+ |
| **U.S. Total** | 8% | 4% | 11% | 11% | 8% | 4% | 12% | 13% | 10% | 4% | 14% | 16% | 12% | 5% | 16% | 20% |
| **Geographic Regions** | | | | | | | | | | | | | | | | |
| New England | 3% | 1% | 5% | 5% | 5% | 2% | 5% | 8% | 5% | 1% | 5% | 11% | 7% | 3% | 9% | 13% |
| Middle Atlantic | 6% | 1% | 8% | 10% | 6% | 2% | 9% | 8% | 7% | 1% | 12% | 11% | 9% | 1% | 11% | 15% |
| East North Central | 8% | 3% | 12% | 13% | 9% | 3% | 13% | 14% | 9% | 3% | 12% | 16% | 13% | 5% | 18% | 20% |
| West North Central | 15% | 6% | 23% | 18% | 15% | 7% | 23% | 21% | 18% | 6% | 26% | 34% | 18% | 7% | 26% | 32% |
| South Atlantic | 8% | 5% | 9% | 11% | 8% | 3% | 11% | 12% | 10% | 3% | 12% | 18% | 13% | 5% | 16% | 20% |
| East South Central | 16% | 11% | 20% | 17% | 16% | 8% | 21% | 25% | 16% | 7% | 22% | 25% | 20% | 10% | 25% | 31% |
| West South Central | 11% | 7% | 16% | 12% | 11% | 7% | 14% | 15% | 14% | 9% | 19% | 18% | 17% | 9% | 22% | 25% |
| Mountain | 9% | 4% | 11% | 16% | 11% | 3% | 16% | 24% | 13% | 3% | 18% | 27% | 15% | 6% | 22% | 30% |
| Pacific | 4% | 2% | 6% | 5% | 4% | 2% | 6% | 8% | 5% | 2% | 7% | 9% | 7% | 3% | 9% | 12% |
| **Gender** | | | | | | | | | | | | | | | | |
| Male | 13% | 6% | 17% | 17% | 14% | 6% | 19% | 21% | 17% | 6% | 23% | 27% | 20% | 8% | 27% | 31% |
| Female | 3% | 2% | 5% | 4% | 3% | 2% | 4% | 3% | 3% | 1% | 4% | 3% | 4% | 3% | 5% | 5% |
| **Ethnicity** | | | | | | | | | | | | | | | | |
| Non-Hispanic | 9% | 5% | 13% | 12% | 9% | 4% | 13% | 14% | 11% | 4% | 15% | 17% | 13% | 6% | 18% | 21% |
| Hispanic | 3% | 1% | 4% | 4% | 3% | 1% | 4% | 5% | 3% | 2% | 3% | 7% | 4% | 2% | 5% | 8% |
| **Race** | | | | | | | | | | | | | | | | |
| White | 10% | 5% | 13% | 13% | 10% | 4% | 14% | 15% | 12% | 4% | 16% | 19% | 14% | 6% | 19% | 23% |
| Non-White | 2% | 1% | 3% | 4% | 2% | 1% | 3% | 3% | 4% | 2% | 4% | 6% | 4% | 2% | 5% | 6% |
| **Annual Household Income (2005 dollars)** | | | | | | | | | | | | | | | | |
| Under $25,000 | 4% | 2% | 6% | 7% | NA | NA | NA | NA | 7% | 2% | 11% | 14% | NA | NA | NA | NA |
| $25,000-$39,999 | 7% | 4% | 10% | 11% | NA | NA | NA | NA | 11% | 5% | 15% | 21% | NA | NA | NA | NA |
| $40,000-$99,999 | 11% | 6% | 15% | 15% | NA | NA | NA | NA | 11% | 4% | 16% | 17% | NA | NA | NA | NA |
| $100,000 or More | 9% | 5% | 12% | 14% | NA | NA | NA | NA | 11% | 4% | 14% | 18% | NA | NA | NA | NA |
| **Metropolitan Statistical Area** | | | | | | | | | | | | | | | | |
| Inside MSA in Central City | 4% | 2% | 5% | 5% | 4% | 2% | 6% | 6% | 6% | 2% | 8% | 12% | NA | NA | NA | NA |
| Inside MSA not in Central City | 8% | 4% | 10% | 11% | 8% | 3% | 10% | 12% | 8% | 3% | 10% | 13% | NA | NA | NA | NA |
| Outside MSA | 18% | 9% | 24% | 25% | 18% | 8% | 25% | 26% | 20% | 8% | 27% | 32% | NA | NA | NA | NA |
| **Population Density** | | | | | | | | | | | | | | | | |
| Urban Area | 5% | 2% | 7% | 7% | 5% | 2% | 7% | 9% | 7% | 2% | 9% | 12% | 9% | 4% | 11% | 15% |
| Rural Area | 19% | 10% | 25% | 25% | 17% | 8% | 23% | 25% | 18% | 7% | 24% | 29% | 21% | 8% | 28% | 34% |

NA = Not Available

# Table A-3. Retention Rate* of Hunters by Age and Selected Characteristics: 1990, 1995, 2000, 2005

| | 2005 | | | | | | | 2000 | | | | | | | 1995 | | | | | | | 1990 | | | | | | |
|---|---|---|---|---|---|---|---|---|---|---|---|---|---|---|---|---|---|---|---|---|---|---|---|---|---|---|---|---|
| | Any Age | 16-24 | 25-34 | 35-44 | 45-54 | 55-64 | 65+ | Any Age | 16-24 | 25-34 | 35-44 | 45-54 | 55-64 | 65+ | Any Age | 16-24 | 25-34 | 35-44 | 45-54 | 55-64 | 65+ | Any Age | 16-24 | 25-34 | 35-44 | 45-54 | 55-64 | 65+ |
| **U.S. Total** | 43% | 74% | 55% | 50% | 43% | 33% | 20% | 43% | 76% | 59% | 53% | 40% | 31% | 18% | 45% | 79% | 60% | 51% | 43% | 34% | 20% | 49% | 79% | 62% | 52% | 44% | 35% | 21% |
| **Geographic Regions** | | | | | | | | | | | | | | | | | | | | | | | | | | | | |
| New England | 38% | 73% | 46% | 46% | 42% | 32% | 20% | 41% | 82% | 57% | 50% | 38% | 29% | 20% | 45% | 83% | 62% | 50% | 43% | 35% | 22% | 46% | 82% | 58% | 46% | 41% | 32% | 23% |
| Middle Atlantic | 47% | 71% | 62% | 59% | 48% | 36% | 25% | 49% | 82% | 61% | 60% | 41% | 39% | 26% | 50% | 88% | 57% | 58% | 47% | 39% | 21% | 54% | 85% | 66% | 55% | 48% | 40% | 27% |
| East North Central | 47% | 76% | 63% | 54% | 51% | 35% | 22% | 47% | 85% | 66% | 60% | 41% | 31% | 20% | 49% | 81% | 63% | 56% | 45% | 32% | 21% | 51% | 81% | 65% | 53% | 43% | 33% | 21% |
| West North Central | 50% | 76% | 64% | 56% | 54% | 39% | 24% | 52% | 84% | 71% | 62% | 47% | 37% | 24% | 53% | 84% | 71% | 59% | 48% | 38% | 25% | 52% | 81% | 66% | 58% | 44% | 40% | 19% |
| South Atlantic | 40% | 74% | 54% | 46% | 37% | 32% | 16% | 40% | 70% | 56% | 49% | 37% | 30% | 17% | 40% | 75% | 53% | 44% | 39% | 31% | 16% | 48% | 78% | 60% | 49% | 44% | 33% | 20% |
| East South Central | 46% | 76% | 59% | 57% | 45% | 34% | 22% | 48% | 84% | 66% | 52% | 44% | 32% | 18% | 51% | 81% | 65% | 56% | 44% | 34% | 25% | 55% | 85% | 69% | 58% | 50% | 36% | 26% |
| West South Central | 47% | 80% | 53% | 57% | 43% | 39% | 25% | 46% | 78% | 56% | 50% | 46% | 34% | 20% | 49% | 72% | 66% | 54% | 46% | 34% | 24% | 54% | 75% | 63% | 60% | 49% | 41% | 26% |
| Mountain | 36% | 62% | 50% | 40% | 38% | 26% | 16% | 42% | 70% | 53% | 47% | 44% | 26% | 16% | 45% | 79% | 56% | 46% | 42% | 38% | 21% | 50% | 75% | 61% | 53% | 44% | 38% | 22% |
| Pacific | 27% | 63% | 40% | 32% | 27% | 23% | 10% | 28% | 51% | 43% | 42% | 23% | 19% | 11% | 33% | 67% | 45% | 36% | 35% | 28% | 12% | 36% | 66% | 46% | 40% | 35% | 24% | 14% |
| **Gender** | | | | | | | | | | | | | | | | | | | | | | | | | | | | |
| Male | 44% | 74% | 58% | 53% | 45% | 35% | 22% | 46% | 78% | 62% | 55% | 42% | 34% | 22% | 48% | 81% | 62% | 53% | 45% | 35% | 21% | 52% | 81% | 64% | 54% | 46% | 37% | 23% |
| Female | 33% | 72% | 43% | 39% | 31% | 22% | 8% | 32% | 65% | 44% | 41% | 29% | 16% | 8% | 33% | 63% | 46% | 37% | 28% | 24% | 13% | 38% | 66% | 51% | 42% | 33% | 24% | 12% |
| **Ethnicity** | | | | | | | | | | | | | | | | | | | | | | | | | | | | |
| Non-Hispanic | 42% | 74% | 56% | 50% | 43% | 33% | 20% | 44% | 77% | 60% | 53% | 40% | 31% | 20% | 45% | 79% | 60% | 51% | 43% | 34% | 20% | 49% | 79% | 62% | 52% | 44% | 35% | 21% |
| Hispanic | 45% | 61% | 53% | 49% | 44% | 40% | 15% | 43% | 64% | 44% | 52% | 36% | 25% | 8% | 45% | 72% | 55% | 45% | 33% | 25% | 25% | 53% | 64% | 58% | 60% | 42% | 35% | 24% |
| **Race** | | | | | | | | | | | | | | | | | | | | | | | | | | | | |
| White | 43% | 74% | 57% | 51% | 44% | 33% | 20% | 44% | 77% | 59% | 54% | 40% | 32% | 20% | 46% | 79% | 61% | 51% | 43% | 34% | 20% | 50% | 79% | 62% | 53% | 45% | 35% | 21% |
| Non-White | 33% | 66% | 41% | 43% | 28% | 28% | 17% | 33% | 61% | 50% | 38% | 29% | 22% | 14% | 39% | 78% | 49% | 42% | 37% | 25% | 14% | 41% | 67% | 54% | 43% | 34% | 32% | 21% |
| **Annual Household Income (2000 dollars)** | | | | | | | | | | | | | | | | | | | | | | | | | | | | |
| Under $25,000 | 31% | 61% | 44% | 42% | 31% | 26% | 15% | 34% | 66% | 51% | 40% | 30% | 21% | 13% | 34% | 66% | 43% | 48% | 28% | 30% | 19% | NA | NA | NA | NA | NA | NA | NA |
| $25,000-$39,999 | 41% | 68% | 54% | 55% | 36% | 34% | 17% | 47% | 73% | 65% | 51% | 39% | 37% | 22% | 47% | 73% | 65% | 51% | 39% | 37% | 22% | NA | NA | NA | NA | NA | NA | NA |
| $40,000-$99,999 | 48% | 78% | 59% | 49% | 49% | 35% | 26% | 49% | 82% | 62% | 64% | 36% | 35% | 19% | 49% | 82% | 62% | 52% | 45% | 35% | 19% | NA | NA | NA | NA | NA | NA | NA |
| $100,000 or More | 47% | 81% | 58% | 51% | 44% | 35% | 28% | 47% | 85% | 58% | 47% | 44% | 34% | 21% | 47% | 85% | 58% | 47% | 44% | 34% | 21% | NA | NA | NA | NA | NA | NA | NA |
| **Metropolitan Statistical Area** | | | | | | | | | | | | | | | | | | | | | | | | | | | | |
| Inside MSA in Central City | 32% | 65% | 38% | 35% | 33% | 27% | 13% | 35% | 63% | 51% | 40% | 30% | 21% | 13% | 37% | 67% | 54% | 38% | 35% | 25% | 14% | NA | NA | NA | NA | NA | NA | NA |
| Inside MSA not in Central City | 42% | 74% | 56% | 50% | 42% | 31% | 18% | 41% | 77% | 56% | 51% | 36% | 29% | 18% | 43% | 77% | 55% | 48% | 39% | 33% | 17% | NA | NA | NA | NA | NA | NA | NA |
| Outside MSA | 51% | 77% | 69% | 60% | 51% | 41% | 23% | 52% | 88% | 69% | 64% | 51% | 40% | 23% | 55% | 87% | 68% | 63% | 54% | 39% | 23% | NA | NA | NA | NA | NA | NA | NA |
| **Population Density** | | | | | | | | | | | | | | | | | | | | | | | | | | | | |
| Urban Area | 35% | 65% | 48% | 42% | 36% | 26% | 14% | 36% | 68% | 52% | 45% | 32% | 26% | 14% | 39% | 73% | 54% | 41% | 37% | 28% | 16% | 43% | 73% | 55% | 44% | 37% | 29% | 17% |
| Rural Area | 53% | 84% | 70% | 61% | 53% | 43% | 28% | 53% | 87% | 69% | 63% | 49% | 42% | 26% | 54% | 85% | 71% | 63% | 50% | 41% | 25% | 59% | 87% | 73% | 64% | 54% | 43% | 28% |

NA= Not Available

Note: Retention Rate is the percent of individuals who have ever hunted that participated in the three years prior to 1991 (1990, 1989, 1988), 1996, 2001, or 2006 Surveys

# Table A-4. Retention Rate* of Anglers by Age and Selected Characteristics: 1990, 1995, 2000, 2005

| | 2005 | | | | | | | 2000 | | | | | | | 1995 | | | | | | | 1990 | | | | | | |
|---|---|---|---|---|---|---|---|---|---|---|---|---|---|---|---|---|---|---|---|---|---|---|---|---|---|---|---|---|
| | Any Age | 16-24 | 25-34 | 35-44 | 45-54 | 55-64 | 65+ | Any Age | 16-24 | 25-34 | 35-44 | 45-54 | 55-64 | 65+ | Any Age | 16-24 | 25-34 | 35-44 | 45-54 | 55-64 | 65+ | Any Age | 16-24 | 25-34 | 35-44 | 45-54 | 55-64 | 65+ |
| **U.S. Total** | 57% | 69% | 65% | 67% | 58% | 50% | 33% | 60% | 73% | 69% | 69% | 58% | 51% | 35% | 61% | 73% | 71% | 69% | 59% | 51% | 36% | 65% | 76% | 73% | 72% | 64% | 55% | 39% |
| **Geographic Regions** | | | | | | | | | | | | | | | | | | | | | | | | | | | | |
| New England | 54% | 65% | 61% | 62% | 56% | 45% | 27% | 57% | 71% | 62% | 66% | 59% | 47% | 31% | 59% | 71% | 68% | 68% | 55% | 45% | 35% | 62% | 73% | 69% | 67% | 60% | 47% | 36% |
| Middle Atlantic | 54% | 63% | 63% | 66% | 52% | 44% | 31% | 57% | 74% | 67% | 65% | 54% | 51% | 30% | 59% | 73% | 66% | 69% | 57% | 46% | 31% | 62% | 75% | 69% | 68% | 59% | 47% | 38% |
| East North Central | 60% | 74% | 67% | 68% | 60% | 53% | 34% | 60% | 73% | 70% | 68% | 57% | 51% | 37% | 63% | 71% | 72% | 71% | 61% | 52% | 37% | 65% | 75% | 72% | 70% | 65% | 54% | 37% |
| West North Central | 63% | 75% | 70% | 73% | 65% | 59% | 38% | 66% | 81% | 78% | 79% | 62% | 53% | 42% | 66% | 75% | 73% | 75% | 67% | 58% | 39% | 67% | 75% | 77% | 74% | 64% | 63% | 39% |
| South Atlantic | 59% | 72% | 66% | 71% | 60% | 54% | 33% | 63% | 72% | 71% | 74% | 62% | 58% | 38% | 62% | 74% | 73% | 70% | 60% | 52% | 40% | 69% | 80% | 78% | 74% | 67% | 59% | 43% |
| East South Central | 61% | 72% | 73% | 65% | 63% | 53% | 40% | 65% | 76% | 80% | 71% | 65% | 55% | 40% | 65% | 78% | 77% | 71% | 62% | 58% | 37% | 70% | 83% | 79% | 77% | 68% | 60% | 40% |
| West South Central | 61% | 72% | 70% | 72% | 59% | 52% | 38% | 61% | 78% | 73% | 72% | 58% | 49% | 38% | 64% | 72% | 78% | 68% | 63% | 56% | 36% | 70% | 82% | 80% | 77% | 68% | 58% | 42% |
| Mountain | 53% | 63% | 63% | 62% | 54% | 43% | 28% | 58% | 71% | 67% | 64% | 58% | 48% | 28% | 60% | 74% | 69% | 68% | 57% | 53% | 33% | 64% | 74% | 72% | 69% | 60% | 54% | 40% |
| Pacific | 49% | 61% | 52% | 57% | 51% | 42% | 27% | 52% | 67% | 60% | 61% | 50% | 42% | 27% | 54% | 70% | 59% | 61% | 55% | 45% | 26% | 60% | 69% | 67% | 68% | 60% | 52% | 32% |
| **Gender** | | | | | | | | | | | | | | | | | | | | | | | | | | | | |
| Male | 62% | 74% | 68% | 70% | 63% | 56% | 40% | 65% | 78% | 72% | 73% | 64% | 58% | 40% | 67% | 79% | 75% | 74% | 65% | 57% | 42% | 71% | 82% | 78% | 77% | 70% | 61% | 46% |
| Female | 49% | 62% | 60% | 62% | 49% | 39% | 23% | 51% | 64% | 66% | 63% | 49% | 39% | 24% | 52% | 63% | 64% | 62% | 50% | 41% | 25% | 57% | 68% | 68% | 65% | 55% | 47% | 29% |
| **Ethnicity** | | | | | | | | | | | | | | | | | | | | | | | | | | | | |
| Non-Hispanic | 57% | 69% | 65% | 67% | 58% | 50% | 33% | 59% | 73% | 69% | 68% | 58% | 51% | 35% | 61% | 73% | 71% | 69% | 58% | 51% | 36% | 65% | 76% | 73% | 72% | 64% | 55% | 39% |
| Hispanic | 58% | 66% | 63% | 65% | 51% | 46% | 27% | 66% | 73% | 70% | 72% | 59% | 52% | 32% | 65% | 69% | 73% | 66% | 59% | 57% | 32% | 70% | 77% | 73% | 71% | 66% | 64% | 37% |
| **Race** | | | | | | | | | | | | | | | | | | | | | | | | | | | | |
| White | 58% | 70% | 66% | 68% | 58% | 50% | 33% | 60% | 74% | 71% | 70% | 58% | 51% | 35% | 61% | 74% | 71% | 70% | 58% | 51% | 35% | 66% | 77% | 74% | 72% | 64% | 55% | 39% |
| Black | 52% | 61% | 55% | 57% | 53% | 47% | 35% | 53% | 62% | 56% | 59% | 55% | 46% | 35% | 57% | 60% | 62% | 62% | 59% | 53% | 35% | 61% | 71% | 63% | 67% | 61% | 56% | 38% |
| Other | 49% | 60% | 54% | 55% | 48% | 37% | 23% | 58% | 65% | 64% | 58% | 54% | 56% | 38% | 63% | 70% | 69% | 63% | 63% | 48% | 38% | 67% | 69% | 71% | 72% | 65% | 58% | 39% |
| **Annual Household Income (2000 dollars)** | | | | | | | | | | | | | | | | | | | | | | | | | | | | |
| Under $25,000 | 51% | 68% | 68% | 65% | 49% | 45% | 27% | 54% | 68% | 61% | 62% | 51% | 42% | 29% | 53% | 70% | 72% | 62% | 52% | 45% | 32% | NA | NA | NA | NA | NA | NA | NA |
| $25,000-$39,999 | 56% | 65% | 64% | 68% | 54% | 47% | 37% | 60% | 74% | 69% | 68% | 58% | 51% | 34% | 61% | 71% | 71% | 68% | 63% | 53% | 37% | NA | NA | NA | NA | NA | NA | NA |
| $40,000-$99,999 | 62% | 71% | 66% | 68% | 60% | 53% | 41% | 65% | 78% | 81% | 79% | 63% | 56% | 40% | 65% | 75% | 71% | 70% | 61% | 55% | 41% | NA | NA | NA | NA | NA | NA | NA |
| $100,000 or More | 62% | 69% | 64% | 68% | 61% | 53% | 44% | 64% | 75% | 82% | 78% | 64% | 53% | 44% | 64% | 75% | 68% | 70% | 60% | 53% | 40% | NA | NA | NA | NA | NA | NA | NA |
| **Metropolitan Statistical Area** | | | | | | | | | | | | | | | | | | | | | | | | | | | | |
| Inside MSA in Central City | 49% | 59% | 57% | 58% | 48% | 41% | 25% | 54% | 61% | 62% | 62% | 51% | 42% | 29% | 55% | 69% | 64% | 62% | 51% | 47% | 29% | NA | NA | NA | NA | NA | NA | NA |
| Inside MSA not in Central City | 58% | 71% | 66% | 68% | 59% | 50% | 34% | 60% | 69% | 68% | 68% | 58% | 51% | 34% | 61% | 71% | 71% | 69% | 60% | 49% | 33% | NA | NA | NA | NA | NA | NA | NA |
| Outside MSA | 64% | 76% | 76% | 75% | 65% | 59% | 39% | 65% | 78% | 79% | 79% | 63% | 56% | 40% | 68% | 81% | 81% | 77% | 68% | 58% | 43% | NA | NA | NA | NA | NA | NA | NA |
| **Population Density** | | | | | | | | | | | | | | | | | | | | | | | | | | | | |
| Urban Area | 54% | 66% | 61% | 63% | 54% | 45% | 29% | 56% | 70% | 65% | 65% | 55% | 46% | 31% | 58% | 70% | 69% | 65% | 55% | 49% | 31% | 62% | 74% | 70% | 68% | 61% | 52% | 35% |
| Rural Area | 66% | 78% | 78% | 75% | 66% | 59% | 43% | 67% | 81% | 82% | 78% | 67% | 59% | 43% | 67% | 79% | 76% | 78% | 68% | 56% | 43% | 72% | 83% | 82% | 78% | 70% | 63% | 47% |

NA= Not Available

Note: Retention Rate is the percent of individuals who have ever hunted that participated in the three years prior to 1991 (1990, 1989, 1988), 1996, 2001, or 2006 Surveys

## Table A-5. Logit Regression Explanatory Variables

**USDAYS_H**  
Continuous variable for the number of days spent hunting by the male parent of a child residing at home

**INCOME**  
Ordinal variable with 10 levels, treated as continuous

> Under $10,000
>
> $10-$19,999
>
> $20-$24,999
>
> $25-$29,999
>
> $30-$34,999
>
> $35-$39,999
>
> $40-$49,999
>
> $50-$74,999
>
> $75-$99,999
>
> $100,000 or More

**HISPANIC**  
Indicator variable with 2 values to indicate ethnicity

> Not Hispanic
>
> Hispanic

**MSA_URBAN**  
Nominal variable with 3 levels to indicate population density of residence

> Rural
>
> Urban with less than one million residents
>
> Urban with greater than or equal to one million residents

**PUBLIC**  
Indicator variable with 2 values to indicate whether individual hunted on private or public land

> Hunted on at least some private land
>
> Hunted only on public land

**LEASE**  
Indicator variable with 2 values to indicate whether individual leased hunting land

> Did not lease hunting land
>
> Leased hunting land

**SPECIES_SQUIRREL**  
Indicator variable with 2 values to indicate whether individual hunted squirrel

> Did not hunt
>
> Hunted

**SPECIES_TURKEY**  
Indicator variable with 2 values to indicate whether individual hunted turkey

> Did not hunt
>
> Hunted

**SPECIES_QUAIL**  
Indicator variable with 2 values to indicate whether individual hunted quail

> Did not hunt
>
> Hunted

**SPECIES_GROUSE**  
Indicator variable with 2 values to indicate whether individual hunted grouse

> Did not hunt
>
> Hunted

**SPECIES_DOVE**  
Indicator variable with 2 values to indicate whether individual hunted dove

> Did not hunt
>
> Hunted

## Table A-6. Analysis of Maximum Likelihood Estimates of Logit Regression

| Variable | Value | Estimate | Standard Error | Chi-Square | Pr > ChiSq |
|---|---|---|---|---|---|
| Intercept | | −1.147 | 0.221 | 26.9 | <.0001 |
| USDAYS_H | | 0.018 | 0.004 | 24.7 | <.0001 |
| INCOME | | 0.058 | 0.028 | 4.4 | 0.037 |
| HISPANIC | Hispanic | −0.620 | 0.345 | 3.2 | 0.072 |
| MSA_URBAN | Urban with < one million residents | −0.185 | 0.142 | 1.7 | 0.193 |
| MSA_URBAN | Urban with ≥ one million residents | −0.469 | 0.163 | 8.3 | 0.004 |
| PUBLIC | Hunted only on public land | −0.552 | 0.176 | 9.8 | 0.002 |
| LEASE | Lease hunting land | −0.730 | 0.217 | 11.3 | 0.001 |
| SPECIES_SQUIRREL | Hunted | 0.599 | 0.158 | 14.4 | 0.000 |
| SPECIES_TURKEY | Hunted | 0.393 | 0.153 | 6.6 | 0.01 |
| SPECIES_QUAIL | Hunted | −0.410 | 0.219 | 3.5 | 0.061 |
| SPECIES_GROUSE | Hunted | 0.410 | 0.202 | 4.1 | 0.043 |
| SPECIES_DOVE | Hunted | 0.549 | 0.176 | 9.7 | 0.002 |